SUBMARINERS'
NEWS

SUBMARINERS' NEWS

The Peculiar Press of the Underwater Mariner

KEITH HALL

The History Press

All money raised from the sale of this book will be donated to the
Submariners Association West of Scotland branch.

Frontispiece: HMS *Conqueror*'s return fron The Falklands, 1982.

First published 2010

The History Press
The Mill, Brimscombe Port
Stroud, Gloucestershire, GL5 2QG
www.thehistorypress.co.uk

British Library Cataloguing in Publication Data.
A catalogue record for this book is available from the British Library.

ISBN 978 0 7524 5793 2

Typesetting and origination by The History Press
Printed in Great Britain

CONTENTS

ALSO BY THE AUTHOR

Around Gareloch and Rosneath Peninsula
ISBN: 978-0-7524-2106-3

HMS Defiance
ISBN: 978-0-7524-3758-3

HMS Dolphin: Gosport's Submarine Base
ISBN: 978-0-7524-2113-1

Gareloch and Rosneath (Pocket Images)
ISBN: 978-1-8458-8402-4

Rosneath and Gareloch: Then and Now
ISBN: 978-0-7524-2389-0

Submariners: Real Life Stories from the Deep
ISBN: 978-0-7524-2809-3

The Clyde Submarine Base: Images of Scotland
ISBN: 978-0-7524-1657-1

ACKNOWLEDGEMENTS

I am very grateful to the following people for their assistance in helping me compile this book:

Andy Ellis, Ron Rietveld and John Lenting. Particular thanks to Tony Smyth for his photos, stories and more importantly his friendship over the years, and not forgetting his daily weather updates from Malta. Also thanks to the members of the West of Scotland Submariners Association for sharing their stories with me, putting up with my endless questions and generally keeping a 'nuclear' boy right.

Special thanks to Ian Moore who carried out research in the RN Submarine Museum archives for me and supplied a few good O boat dits, and the museum itself for permission to use its material.

I am especially indebted to the Babcock Graphic Design Department, Clyde, for contributing to the stunning cover, as well as the design department at The History Press, who helped put this together.

The History Press for once again allowing me to state the submariners' case and in particular my Commissioning Editor Amy Rigg for her help and advice and Miranda Love for making sense of all this and putting the book together. I apologise for the odd rude word that may have escaped the censor's not-so-vigilant pen.

There are undoubtedly many people who have contributed to this book who I have failed to acknowledge, primarily the submarine crews themselves. I apologise and thank you all and hope none of the content offends.

Finally, Dangerous McGill and Stir Crazy Fielding for keeping me safe during those long patrols and, of course, the Royal Navy, without whom none of this would have been necessary.

HMS *Renown* under tow.

INTRODUCTION

Imagine a world, a weird world, where 100 people or more live in a metal tube about 300ft long and 40ft in diameter, and because of various pieces of equipment the actual living space is probably not much bigger than a detached house. It is the very stuff of reality television shows; being enclosed for months at a time with a group of people not of your choosing, some of them not even particularly good friends. Constantly light, yet there is no night or day. It is always noisy, and there is very little in the way of privacy. Then the tube is put underwater for months at a time with almost no contact with the outside world. It is a world where you have no option but to rely on your shipmates. It creates special and profound friendships and generates a special relationship between all levels of the crew. Cdr Tall's letter, 'published' in the boats magazine, written when he was leaving HMS *Churchill*, gives an indication of this relationship (see p23).

This is the world of the submariner and to help him cope with it, he has developed a bizarre and undoubtedly distinctive sense of humour. Tales of practical jokes and anecdotes were originally passed by word of mouth, normally accompanied by a pint or two of beer or a tot of rum. In more recent times these stories were recorded in the ship's magazine.

From the earliest days of submarines the crews have used humour as a shield, a safety valve, a relaxation technique and a method of coping with the trials and tribulations of their lives. It is also a convivial way to put wrongs right, or point out the error of someone's ways. No matter where a submariner's head finishes up, his sense of humour – or at least that of his colleagues – ensures his feet will always stay firmly on the floor. People who carried out this job required a resilient sense of humour which manifested itself initially in newsletters and, later, as submarines got bigger and the production methods became more sophisticated, the magazines became more upmarket. But regardless of the era, the method of production or the language, the magazines always showed the submariners' self-deprecating character. The following story illustrates this:

Een autoriteit hield eensvoor vertrek naar zee een toespraak en sprak over the gedenkstenen met Gebeitelde namen, welke bij het nageslacht de namen van de gevallen helden levendig zouden houden.

Nadat weer dieltebommen boot en mens hadden doen sidderen, klonk het plotseling: hoor je ze weer beitelen? See what I mean?

I had a cameo naval role for over thirty years and was involved with boats' magazines for most of this time. From a young boy I ran around knowing I should have been doing something, but wasn't sure what. Until my twilight years, with my Zimmer-assisted shuffle, I was, perhaps, in truth, still not sure of what I was doing. I became involved with magazines on my first submarine, as a straight-out-of-the-box green medical assistant. I found the whole submarine thing fascinating; everything was new, I understood nothing. There were no floors, instead there were decks; walls became bulkheads; ceilings, for some reason, were called deckheads. There were a multitude of water tanks that did all sorts of things apart from holding water, or so it seemed, and strangely the toilets were known as heads.

I should mention at this stage that during my submarine training I had been to sea on an A boat and I knew it required at least a degree in mechanical engineering to work the submarine loo successfully! It must be pointed out that the nuclear submarine toilet was, in comparison, relatively normal, or at least it was until the chief stoker and his staff attempted to repair it. Anyway, not long after joining my first submarine, a Polaris boat, I was in the sickbay when a leading seaman staggered in:

'Doc, me head's killing me!'
'Are you using it right?', I innocently enquired.

The leading seaman left shaking his head, muttering something about OD. I think I single-handedly created a whole new category of ODness, a Leading OD. Needless to say, I made the magazine. I would like to think that over the years I became a little more knowledgeable and developed a certain degree of 'street cred', but if truth were told it was probably just a wishful dream. I left the submarine service much the same as I joined it, totally bewildered and in the dark. So I reasoned, if I was destined to spend much of my career in the magazines, I might as well be in a position where I had some editorial control over the recording of my imprudent actions and inane ramblings. I could airbrush my naval career – or at least that was the plan.

It is a strange fact, but it seems that a large percentage of the magazines were produced by the ships' medical staff, certainly in the latter years of the nuclear submarines. I once discussed this with my very good friend, the chief

Relaxing on the cruising HMS *Renown*.

stoker. I modestly suggested it was probably due to the fact that the medical staff were generally more intelligent, better educated and more articulate than the rest of the crew. 'It's just 'cos you've got bugger all else to do, bloody walking ballast,' was the chief stoker's considered reply. But whatever the truth, the magazines provide a unique insight into the submariners' curious world. Like old newspapers, the ships' magazines give an insight into the past. They stir up memories; tell tales of prior times and perhaps, most importantly, they help us remember old friends. They offer a doorway to the past, admittedly a slightly warped doorway, but nevertheless an enjoyable and amusing one.

The book has been sanitised in so much as the more extreme swear words have been removed. I know it is hard to believe that four-letter words such as 'gosh' would pass a submariner's lips, or the slightly longer 'cor blimey', but unbelievable as it is, uttered they are. Unfortunately the original pages from the magazines are not so easily laundered, so please accept my apologies now.

To ensure readers get the full value from the book each chapter is preceded by a few tips to help you get in the mind of the submariner, to set the scene as it were. Please try them, but make sure there is an adult in the room and, if you do them at home, make sure it is at someone else's house.

So, with great pride and at practically no cost, I present...(fans of the cataclysmic climax will barely be able to contain themselves at this point): *Submariner's News: The Peculiar Press of the Underwater Mariner.*

I hope you will find this book amusing, entertaining and educational, if somewhat disturbing.

Keith Hall
Tumbledown
April 2010

GLOSSARY

AB	Able Seaman
LH	Leading Hand
CC	Charge Chief
Ck	Chief
CPO	Chief Petty Officer
CO	Commanding Officer
DMEO	Deputy Marine Engineering Officer
EOOD	Engineer Officer of the Day
EOOW	Engineer Officer of the Watch
Lt	Lieutenant
MEO	Marine Engineering Officer
MA	Medical Assistant
MC	Missile Compartment
MCC	Missile Control Centre
O Boat	Oberon Class Submarine; a conventional diesel-powered submarine
OOD	Officer of the Day
OOW	Officer of the Watch
PO	Petty Officer
POCk	Petty Officer Chef
SA	Stores Assistant
SCO	Ship Control Officer
SCOW	Ship Control Officer of the Watch
WEO	Weapons Engineering Officer
XO	Executive Officer (1st Lieutenant)

PREAMBLE

Submariners have produced news sheets or magazines for a number of years. Cdr Edward Young produced his, *Good Night* (the *Daily Mirror* produced a paper for submariners called *Good Morning* during the Second World War), while commanding HMS *Storm*. Cdr Young came from a publishing background and returned to it after the war; in fact, he designed the Penguin book logo.

M1 had a magazine and depot ships often produced some form of newsletter. HMS *Oxley* produced a paper called *The OUT Look*. In later years, O boats often produced magazines. *Orpheus* had a paper called *The White Rat*. Members of the crew would drop off a story, in the finest tradition of the service normally anonymously, highlighting funny incidents and cock-ups. As with Cdr Young's paper, it also provided a platform for the captain to inform the crew of what was going on.

REM Jan Ayers, on HMS *Onyx*, produced *Fredzoil* during 1970, while HMS *Oppossum* had the *Ratticus Blanco*.

When I enquired how many copies the boats produced (I belong to the Xerox and computer generation), I was told it depended on how hard you pressed the typewriter keys. Oh for the halcyon days of carbon paper.

However, it was with the coming of the nuclear boats that underwater journalism really came into its own. More space, loads of electricity, Xerox machines and the ubiquitous PC heralded a new golden age of underwater journalism. This gave free reign to the submariners' weird and wonderful sense of humour.

USN *Nautilus*, the world's first nuclear submarine, had a daily newspaper, the name of which was changed every day in keeping with the fast-moving *Nautilus*. It carried the notation: 'Contributions for this sheet are accepted from all hands. No words barred. Do your damnedest. No secrets, we tell all. If you see your name today, use your 'friend's' tomorrow.'

Some samples from this newspaper include:

Latest 'sack time' study by the Executive Officer has our Gunnery Department head logging 19 hours a day, even with the time changes.

'Wanted – Information on why Lt Boyd is aboard. Anyone with information kindly inform Lt Boyd.'

Same the whole world over.

HMS *Dreadnought* had a magazine, unexpectedly dubbed *The Dreadnought Express*. This article appeared in it on 24 September 1967:

NEAR CATASTROPHE AVERTED IN MANOEUVRING ROOM

Prompt action by the ship's Health Physics Staff saved the ship from disaster early yesterday evening. The alarm was raised when it was learnt that all personnel in the Manoeuvring Room had passed out (with the exception of one lone, bearded stalwart). The kiss of life was used to bring them round and soon all was back to normal. Later it was learnt that the Senior Technical Officer had passed his cigarettes round. In the interests of ships Safety, he has promised not to do so again without warning!

A day later:

HEALTH PHYSICS STAFF DENY KISS STORY

A writ was issued today on behalf of the Health Physics Department accusing the *Express* of libel over an article in yesterday's edition. They deny using the kiss of life in the Manoeuvring Room and produced in evidence the fact that no cigarettes have ever been handed around by the Senior Technical Officer. They do state, however, that a box of cigarettes marked 'Happy Christmas 1951' is nearly empty.

I would like to think that the magazines are purely submarine phenomena, and the idea spread through the service as submariners were drafted to newer classes of submarines. But, despite having a well-documented lack of jocularity, several general-service ships also produced magazines. Needless to say, these offerings were not to such a high quality or as exhaustively and comprehensively researched as their underwater counterparts. They also had a complete disregard for the truth, which as any submariner knows is the *raison d'être* for the submariners' magazine.

The illustrations and accompanying text throughout this book, with the exception of the author's tips for the armchair submariner and odd word of explanation, are taken from the various magazines produced by the submariners over the years.

An Ode

(Inspired by a Cup of Cold Cocoa at 0415)

I sing not of Flatfoots or Stokers, of Chippies or Engineers
Who ride triumphantly laurelled across the roster of years,
But of the scorned and rejected—the men hemmed in by fears.

The men of the long night watches which last until they die ;
Dazed with the noonday sun or drowned by a pouring sky,
The men with the aching heads (and often a bloodshot eye).

Not the Flatfoot for me but the Bunting, the tramp of the road,
The slave with a ship on his shoulders pricked on with a goad ;
The man with too weighty a burden, too heavy a load.

The Bunting, the garner of tidings, the fellow that's always about,
Always standing by halliards putting the ships " en route,"
The drowsy chit reporters and the weary bridge lookout.

Others may sing of their jobs, their wealth, and their worth,
But I'll sing a song of a Bunting, he's the salt of the earth.
And he needs the patience of Job from the days of his birth.

HOP. KIN.

(A collection to provide Buntings with halos is *not* receiving our support.—ED.)

Jack's Letter

My dearest of Mothers
This letter I write
On arrival at Wei-hai,
The land of delight.

I am feeling most happy,
Quite healthy and strong
Since leaving that clammy
Isle of Hong Kong.

We arrived at Wei-hai
And were settling down,
When an S.O.S. came
From a North China town.

So we went to the place
('Twas Chefoo by name),
Full of dance halls and ricshas
And fire without flame.

Ashore in this town
I met a maid in distress,
And found this poor girl
Was a Russian Princess.

But princesses in China
Are easy to meet,
Their numbers are legion
In every street.

I arrived back on board
Feeling weary and sore.
My pockets were empty
And my dollars ashore.

So please send some money
As I'm feeling the strain,
For there's always the chance
That we may go again.

F. W.

RNSM Museum.

No.6   G O O D   E V E N I N G   5th January 1944

_____

   We have been patrolling today off Cape St Vincent, whose
light we sighted during the night. Two aircraft, both ours, are
all that has been seen through the periscope. After surfacing we
proceed round the corner towards the Straits, passing Cape Trafalgar
(which gave its name to the battle, not the other way round)... and
we should sight Africa about noon tomorrow morning. We shall, enemy
aircraft permitting, be on the surface all the rest of the way into
Gibraltar, where we are due to arrive at 5 o'clock tomorrow afternoon.

   Last night we sighted the lights of a vessel making for the
coast. To make sure it wasn't a blockade-runner in disguise, I chased
her (doing a Radar shadowing exercise at the same time). As we came
up to her we found her brilliantly illuminated, and the name PORTUGAL
lit up in large white letters. However, we called her up and asked
her who she was and where she was bound. She immediately replied -
in English - "PORTUGUESE SHIP SAO BRAS COURSE FOR LISBON", to which
we replied, friedly-like, "THANK YOU GOOD NIGHT AND GOOD LUCK", at
which she went off into a long message in Portuguese and ended up
with the International Code for "Goodbye and good luck" (or some
such matey phrase). From all of which we deduced that the natives
appear friendly.

   There were more aircraft reports last night of attacks on
U-Boats. As Max Horton said, when he visited "STORM" at Birkenhead,
"You can thank your lucky stars you're not a German submarine!"

   There will be no issue of "Good Evening" tomorrow. Temporary
editorial offices may be set up either in the Capitol, or the Rock
Hotel, or maybe even the Embassy if that snappy little brunette
is still dancing there.   Lieut. Blake thinks not.

                                                        EY.

G O O D   E V E N I N G   4th January 194⎯

                                                         T

     In the early hours of this morning we chased a lighted ship
that turned out to be illuminated as a hospital ship. This was
puzzling, since we have had no signals about our own hospital ship
sailings, and even enemy hospital ships are usually well advertised
to all shipping before sailing. We were unable to overtake her, and
I saw no point in adding grey hairs to the Chief E.R.A's head by doing
a full power trial for the sake of a possibly harmless ship. So I
compromised, abandoned the chase and made a signal to Gibraltar reportin⎯
the ship. She was steering a course for England, so in all probability
she was one of ours, but it seems odd that we weren't informed of
a hospital ship expected to pass through our position.

     Tonight we surface some forty odd miles off the River Tagus, at
the mouth of which, as every schoolboy knows, lies Portugal's capital,
LISBON, a hotbed of international spies whose breeding ground is in
the mass of war refugees who eventually make their way there in the
usually vain hope of getting passage to America. Tonight's run
should end us up a few miles short of Cape St Vincent, and tomorrow's
dive will be the last full day's dive before reaching Gib.

     Our special war correspondent, Richard Dimbleby Blake, reports
an ugly incident which occured when he was last in Lisbon, when a
slightly inebriated member of his party (he himself being completely
sober at the time) remarked to one of the several dizzy blondes
in the party, "And which side are you spying for now?"

     Our gossip writes, "Why is the First Lieutenant dressed up
to the nines tonight? Has he had a buzz from the Coxswain that we
are putting in to Lisbon tonight?" (If No.1 thinks that Captain S.4
would be impressed by the addition of a couple of Lisbon international
spy blondes to his F.O.S. Shipment, he is labouring under a misappreh-
ension. - Capt.) ("I'd much rather be labouring under one of those
blondes." - 1st. Lieut.)

     What is all this about blondes?

G O O D   E V E N I N G   3rd January 1944

*   *   *   *   *   *   *   *   *   *   *

Sorry I had to disappoint all you bloodthirsty pirates today, but we are not at war with Spain yet, and this is too early in my naval career to face a court-martial. Our target turned out to be the Spanish CAPITAN SEGARRA of 2252 tons. She is in my list of neutral ships that are above suspicion. Anyway, we went up close enough to read her name and make sure she couldn't have been a blockade runner in disguise. It made a change, at any rate.

We are now gradually closing in towards the Portuguese coast. It is possible we might see the glow of the lights of Lisbon during tonight. Ships encountered from now on are more likely than not to be neutral, though these naturally will have their lights burning, and any darkened ship is just asking for one of the T.I's death-dealing fish. And of course anywhere on the ocean these days we are always likely to meet U-Boats. We are a little ahead of our schedule, and will have to proceed slowly in order to keep within our bombing restriction.

From last night's signal log:-
From A/C RCNF to BASE: "AM OVER ENEMY SUBMARINE IN POSITION
    45 55 N 07 55 W.........0012."
From A/C RCNF to BASE: "MY 0012. HAVE ATTACKED ENEMY SUBMARINE
    WITH DEPTH CHARGES AND ESTIMATE HITS PROBABLE..... 0020."

(TO BE RETURNED TO ME - Captain)

RNSM Museum.

G O O D   E V E N I N G   2nd January 1944

Star and sun sights have confirmed our dead reckoning position within a few miles. We are now 120 miles West of the coast of Portugal, on the same latitude as Oporto, where the port comes from ("Hard-a-port" says No.1 - ouch!). Any time now the look-outs should be able to smell the scented breezes coming off the land. No.1 sighted a swallow through the periscope today, and yesterday afternoon the Engineer Officer sighted an old boot. These thrilling sightings have prompted the navigator to believe that land can't be far away now.

Coastal Command aircraft were busy in the Bay last night. One sighted a medium-sized merchant vessel steering 280, speed 12 knots, out of the Bay. There were at least five reports from aircraft that they were "Over enemy submarine in position so-and-so." One plaintive signal read "Submarine has disappeared". Dear, dear. There was no news, however, of what happened to the merchant vessel (who may have been a blockade runner) or to the submarines who didn't disappear. In the midst of all this activity on W/T there came a signal from F.O.S. to C-in-C Plymouth: "Owing to extreme congestion of accomodation at Fort Blockhouse request permission for SHAKESPEARE to proceed to Plymouth on arrival." As the Engineer Officer rightly suggested, Blockhouse must have at least two submarines in, in that case. However, the week-end will be along very shortly, when no doubt accomodation will be eased.

*   *   *   *   *   *

CHOOSE YOUR DATE FOR THE SECOND FRONT SWEEPSTAKE

Engineer Officer's Tips Straight from the Horses' Mouth

Every Man His Own Staff Officer. The Engineer Officer has been gathering hints and tips from the Nautical Almanac, Old Moore's Almanac, the Trim Book, the rough (very rough) Engine Room Register, K.R. & A.I., and a study of the heavenly bodies (Jane's included), for the benefit of those who wish to enter this momentous sweepstake on the date of the Second Front with their eyes open. Some say carrots for night vision. I say Nuts. Anyway, here are Chief's hints:

The Moon. The obvious time for an invasion is when there is no moon. Dates on which there will be no moon:-
      January 25th.   February 24th.   March 24th.
On the other hand, these are obviously the dates when the enemy will be expecting invasion. The thing to do is to catch him by surprise. The time he will be most surprised will be when the moon is full, as nobody would expect to invade then. Dates of full moons:-
      January 10th.   February 9th.   March 10th.

Sun. But stay, what do we find is happening on January 25th? Nothing less than a total eclipse of the sun. Total eclipses don't happen every day. Can there be any significance in this?
      On the other hand, on March 21st a very important event occurs. The Sun enters the sign of Aries. What this means we haven't the faintest idea, except that it means the beginning of Spring proper. The Engineer Officer points to the significant word Aries - obviously some connection with Aryans. (I think this smells. - Capt.)

Other pointers to the invasion date are:-
      St. Patrick's Day (when the Irish get fighting mad)

Seargant Ruggles reports for duty .... Feb. 4th
    Capt. Ryan (what a man!) returns to England...... Jan 5th
    Stoker Harris has s sister who is engaged to a Combined Hop
who says they must be married before Feb. 15th
    The First Lieutenant, after prolonged study of the "little
book" says that under Organisation 24c, para. 5G, everything
points to March 2nd. His other suggestion is - look out for
Saturday nights. The African landings were made on a Saturday
night, but then I wouldn't know anything about the habits of
French officers on Saturday nights.

DAILY NAP - ALL THE LEADING TIPSTERS

    Capt. (Times)...... March 15th (the Ides of March, the day o
                                          Caesar's doom)
    No.1 (Irish Northern Whig) March 12th (Inside dope from
                                          Combined Ops)
    Torps. (Jockey)   ????????? (Quarterlies due)
    Navigator (Post) February 24th   (A supporter of the obviou
                                   false no-moon theory)
    Eng. Officer (Herald) March 6th   (His birthday)

Well, there's all the information spread out for you. Take
your choice, boys.

                                                        EM.

        (TO BE RETURNED TO ME)

G O O D   E V E N I N G   1st January 1944

++

We have so far had no star sight since leaving England, but by dead reckoning we have now passed the Bay of Biscay. Considering the time of the year, and the Bay's reputation for making hardened mariners sick, we have been extraordinarily lucky with the weather.

We are now just over a hundred miles due west of Cape Finisterre, xx the north-west corner of Spain. We received our onward route to Gibraltar last night, and from about midnight onwards we steer in a bit towards the Portugese coast to make a point about 20 miles off Cape St. Vincent on the evening of the 5th. After that we shall be on the surface the rest of the way. We are due to arrive Gibraltar at 1700 on the 6th.

U-BOATS. Tonight's disposition signal (based presumably on D/F estimations) indicates sixteen U-Boats either inward or outward bound. Positions are very approximate, and some may quite easily be encountered in our present position.

BLOCKADE RUNNERS. There is no information about any blockade runner in our vicinity at the moment, but this is a favourite area for them in their southern approach to the Bay, and it is always possible that one or two get this far without being spotted.

In yesterday's "Good Evening" I referred to a search being carried out for one of our own aircraft dinghies not far off K.14's route. The dinghy was found yesterday evening by a Sunderland. The story is best told by repeating the signals exchanged between the aircraft and base:-

     2130, Aircraft to Base. "In position over dinghy with aircrew.
       Position 22.30 Where may I land."
     2141, Aircraft to Base. "Surface vessels diverted to reach dinghy.
       Returning to base for fuel."
     2200, Base to Aircraft. "Will surface vessels reach dinghy before
       your prudent limit of endurance. Land at base or Mountbatten
    if you need.".
       The aircraft was now ordered by base to drop markers, and another aircraft was sent to take over. This second aircraft, at 0310 this morning was able to report, "Over dinghy in position, accompanied by ship." And at 0358 base signalled the aircraft, "Action from ship - rescue effected and reported."

A nice piece of co-operation between aircraft and surface vessels.

EH.

(THIS CONTAINS INFORMATION CLASSIFIED AS "SECRET" AND IS TO BE RETURNED TO ME BEFORE THE ISSUE OF THE NEXT BULLETIN).

SECRET.   **No. 14.**   **PRICELESS.**

FEBRUARY.

... The ...

Maidstone Magazine

With which is incorporated "Pandora Piffle"
and "The Alecto Argus.")

CONTENTS.

1. Editorial.
2. Notice.
3. Puss! Puss!!
4. Celebrities in the Periscope No. 14.
5. Tales from Turkey.
6. Niobe—all Smiles.
7. Society Letter by "Miss Astern."
8. Harpings from Holland.
9. The Diary of Samuel Pepys.
10. H.M.S. "Alecto" Letter.

EDITORIAL.

THIS month we have the privilege of submitting works by new and distinguished authors. One correspondent has arrived in Holland, and has taken up his abode at the Hague. Although he has not actually dined with the Kaiser, he has had supper with the Moncreiffe. Mr. Clarkson has sent us a criticism of the Play which is so flattering to the performers, that we expect them to order all our spare copies to send to their best enemies. Our Mediterranean Correspondent sends us four stories which alone are worth the money. Miss Astern, a lady of good family and obviously a keen observer, gives us peeps into the social life of the

19

neighbourhood, and from another point of view we have the "Pepys" of Samuel. We welcome these new contributors, and like Oliver Twist, we ask for more.

THE STAFF.

Next month: "The man who supped with the Moncreiffe." A thrilling psychological study!

NOTICE.

THE total amount of "Maidstone's War Sweep," when Fifth Pool tickets are paid in, will be £193 10s. 0d., not £192 15s. 0d. as shown in "Result of Draw" recently issued. It has been proposed in view of the growing size of the Pool that there should be three Prizes instead of one only. The holder of the ticket with the winning date will receive 75 % and those with tickets immediately on either side of the winning date will receive 12½ % each.

It will be presumed that this proposal meets with general approval if no serious objections are lodged by 31st March next. Those received on the first of the following month will not be regarded as serious.

PUSS! PUSS!!

IT is not true that the Pandora officers come over to light their cigarettes at "Maidstone's" candle.

WHAT we say is, every man his own matches—and Notepaper. This is the spirit that makes England what it is.

THE young lady at Harrods' who asked after "the

RNSM Museum.

The editor has kindly asked me to furnish the opening lines to this the third edition of the THUMPER, which is for me, sadly, my last opportunity to feature in this excellent organ of the ship's company. Talking of organs, can anyone onboard (stand fast the fifth watch) find theirs? Mine seems to have disappeared altogether!

After 33 months in Command, I have of course an abundance of memories and when I bounce my grandchildren on my knee (which could be this year by the way my eldest sons are performing!) I will have a huge fund of dits to spin them about the boat, the runs ashore, the hangovers, the amazing feats of daring, the hundreds of thousands of miles travelled, the elation and at times, sadness, and yes, on occasions, the foot stamping frustration (for those who didn't know why its called the THUMPER).

The lasting memories though will be about people, for it is you lot that make the boat what it is and have earned for her the justified reputation for being the best there is. Keep it that way.

I will leave the humour to the pages that follow and end with a simple message. Thankyou one and all for the fantastic support you have given me during my time in HMS CHURCHILL and for the kindness you have always shown Bonnie. She above anyone in the world knows that this black harbinger of death, and Britain's finest, is going to be a hard act to follow.

Thumper, HMS *Churchill.*

Good luck in the future
and good hunting!

Jeff Tan.

HMS *Renown* (first commission).

The New Black TinFish

issue n⁰ 2

Shock Defeat in Parish Uckers Championships.

A stunned, capacity crowd watched the unpresidented defeat of the self confessed village 'uckers' champions, Budding and Libby, in a 2 : 0 anhialation by the previousely unseeded Lovett and Nichols.

A visibly shaken Mr Budding told our sports reporter "I've been playing this game for 22 years and never in my 22 years of 22 years playing experience have I experienced anything like that. Well not in the last 22 years anyway, One gets to know a thing or two in 22 years but nothing in my 22 years experience could cope with the sure-footed tactics of those two young boys."

It is believed that Mr Budding is closing his board and hanging up his counters and moving north where he hopes to open a golf boutique, which will be named "Billy's Balls".

condensed from the
"Readers Digest"

I am John's Ovaries
(he's had a bad week

Mysterious Illness Sweeps Village

Local health officials met, yesterday, in order to issue a joint statement in an attempt toquell the rising tide of panic as the toll from the so far unidentified virus rises.

Symptoms vary, but most people report vague abdominal discomfort, and nausea. One or two people have also reported that their hairline is receeding, the worst affected, so far, is Mr BW Budding the local 'uckers' champion, whos hairline has receeded back to his 5th lumbar vertebra.

At the meeting Dr Quentin McDonald spoke at some length urging a logical and calm approach to the problem and dismissed, out of hand, rumours that the lack of food in tha diet was the cause. he went on to explain, that in the opinion of the Health Council, the symptoms were of a psycological nature and had little or nothing to do with conditions in the parish at the moment.

It has been admitted, some researchers that a possible cause in many cases could be worry or concern over Scotlands likely early departure from the 'World Cup' fixture list.

Cleverly put....."we are on our way, heading in the general direction of the way we are going."

Are there any volunteers for the, soon to be vacant position, of Navigator.

HMS *Conqueror* (1981).

Editorial Pledge; Absolutely no paper was used
in the production of this Mag.

ISSUE No 2

RESOLUTION REVIEW

©Calgraphics©

PAPERGATE!

Sub-surface Scandal: Sub Skipper to be Subpoena-ed!

Leading Writer points finger at Back-afties!

Despite repeated denials from the 'Bun House', speculation is growing, that senior officials may be implicated in a massive fraud which involves the miss-appropriation of thousands of sheets of Xerox paper.

During a dawn raid on the basement apartment, on 3 deck, of the Leading Writist, Mr. J. Frost,37, told our reporter, prior to being bundled into a police car," It's the Back-afties!They've got it.They're not pinning this bastard on me!"

This reporter can disclose that the standard practice of making recordings of all conversations, with a view to future use against selected parties, for whatever gain, may have become a two-edged sword.

Inasmuch as the recordings may contain certain incriminating statements, that implicates high officials in positions of trust.

There are, however, one or two minor setbacks,namely the vast amount of expletives to be deleted, and due to economic policies, the recording equipment used was not fitted with an AGC.

Consequently there are a lot of 'overloaded ' recordings. Rest assured, Joe Public, if there's anything left, between the Bleeps and the Blurts, all will be revealed.

"WHAT BLOODY PAPER?"

HMS *Resolution.*

ISSUE Nº 1

**THE
REPULSE
RAG**

CENSORED

by James Lycon, RN

HMS *Repulse.*

RESOLUTION REVIEW

©Calgraphics©

**THE THINKING MAN'S
READERS DIGEST**

PETAL PANIC SWEEPS PARISH

Local Health Officials met yesterday in order to issue a joint statement in an attempt to quell the rising tide of panic as the toll from the so far unidentified illness rises.

The symptoms of this illness vary, but most people report discomfort, a slight but noticable green tint, and a strange liking for standing in the showers with their arms held out. Mr A D P Edwards (27) removed his EBS mask to stress that there was absolutely no problem with the village's atmosphere, and that parishioners should carry on with their usual routines as normal.

Also present at the meeting Dr Quentin Parker (42½) spoke at some length, urging a calm and logical approach to the problem, and dismissed out of hand, rumours that a high carbon Dioxide levels were the cause. He went on to explain, ad nauseum that in the opinion of the Health Council, the symptoms were of a Psychological nature and had little or nothing to do with the conditons prevailing in the Parish at the moment.

The meeting was closed by Squire Avery who suggested that the confusion may have arose after a throw away remark he made at the village New Year's Ball, when he likened Mr S Irvine to a Pansy and that Parishoners should not read too much into the new Pipe of "BUTTERCUP, DAISY, W.T.OFFICE"

He also pointed out that if, in the unlikely event, that the crew were turning into plants, the benefits would be tremendous, As the crew would then Photosynthise instead of eat, therefore the Victualling Account savings would be significant. At this point Mr Horace Dowle (61) informed the meeting that he had enough metal polish on board to produce 4050ft³ of ammonia, sufficient to feed a crew of 4 acres for 20 weeks. The Squire then closed the meeting with a reminder to all Divisional Officers to prune and spray their divisions by early Spring and to protect them from early frosts.

KIPPER RIPPER STRIKES AGAIN

Resolution's Crime Squad detectives took the unprecedented step of issuing a public warning (to the public no less) yesterday. D.S.Castledine told reporters that a homicidal maniac was loose on the manor and householders were advised to lock up their fish. The killer who has become known as the Kipper Ripper" last struck at the S.R.Lounge Bar, a small inn just off the green. A distraught Miss Brenda Goodall(86) told our reporter " It was 'orrible, I came to work on Sunday morning, and there they were Dead, even the frogs" at this point Miss Goodall became hysterical and had to be led away by friends (stand fast Andy Gibney). D.S.Castledine said that this attack was typical of the "Kipper's" modu operandi and that he would not rest until he's behind the Bar, eh........ behind bars. Police surgeon Dr. theodore Paker (51) has built up a pschological profile of the villain, which is that he is about 6ft 3in, ginger hair skinhead style cut, and he has probably got a pronounced mechanical bent (bent what......ED) and is most likely to be called BOB.

The crew are advised not to approach this man as he's probably armed and dangerous. Any information should be phoned directly to the crime squad on 240 confidentiality assured.

HMS *Resolution.*

Chapter One

NEWS

TIPS ON HOW TO BE A SUBMARINER:

- Invite as many people as you can to your house, lock the doors and cover the windows so no one can see out. Ensure that some of your guests have personal hygiene problems. Assign everybody a task and insist they log the results, every hour. For added realism, get them to report the results to you. Bollock every third person, no reason is required.

- Ensure that every room in your house is drastically different in temperature. If no condensation appears when you open a door, the temperature difference is not great enough. Check for certain that your bedroom only has two temperatures – 100°F or 20°F – and nothing in between. Ensure there are hourly temperature cycles throughout the night.

- Paint numbers and letters on every button, valve, tap and switch in the house. Force all of the guests to memorise them all, threaten to stop them from leaving if they cannot walk through the house blindfolded naming each item along with its correct usage and number. Some of the numbering should be unreadable to ensure authenticity.

- Put on the headphones from your stereo (do not plug them in). Go and stand in front of your cooker. Shout 'Cooker manned and ready'. Stand there for three or four hours. Shout 'Cooker secured'. Roll up the headphones cord and put them away. For extra effect get your wife to repeat everything you have said, starting each sentence with 'Roger', i.e. 'Roger, cooker manned and ready'.

- Every so often, yell 'Angles and Dangles', run into the kitchen and push all pots/pans/dishes off the worktop onto the floor. Then yell at your wife for not having the place secured for sea.

Far be it for the parish magazine to pass moral judgement but we feel duty bound to draw the following statements to the squire's attention.

During a heated discussion about WRNS on boats:

CC O: 'Imagine 150 blokes and twenty WRNS.'
SA T: 'Yeah, and let's face it, some of them blokes are quite ****able.'
SA T (TO MA D): 'Come and jump on here for some practice.'

As reported in an earlier edition, the aforementioned SA was heard to say outside the wardroom: 'I like bottom.' And after the young SA's performance in the SODS OPERA, well, need we say more? The case for the prosecution rests.

Control Room's very own white rodent, with his latest stunning revelations from this, the very nerve centre of the submarine. Our first report concerns our much maligned (but ever so nice really, POTS), who, while talking to the TASO, was heard to casually warble, 'I was going to bring my blusher and my eye shadow, but I thought the Cox'n was bringing his.' Hmmm.

Rodent's thoughts; has this got anything to do with last week's stunning revelations? Will the hirsute 'Voice' be jealous of the POTS's obviously intimate relationship with the Cox'n?

Our next disclosure relates to the SCO who, we can tell, is destined to adorn our pages with increasing frequency:

SCO snatches up phone and dials 233.

SCO: 'Hello MC, SCO here, has anybody made a loud whooshing noise in the MC recently?' The MC's reply was totally garbled and muffled hysterics.

Our last exclusive report highlights the high degree of Control Room etiquette that we have come to know and love, and concerns the supply officer at ship control, and, yet again, SCO as OOW.

Our story begins at the watch handover, when the supply officer spots a whisky tumbler on the bookshelf. He frantically makes furtive whispered enquiries of the console watch keeper and the planesmen as to who owns the glass. Receiving negative responses from both and becoming increasingly agitated he turns to the SCO, who is standing about 3ft away, and looking directly at him says:

Supply Officer:	'OOW, Ship Control.'
SCO:	'Oh for ****'s sake.'
Supply Officer:	'OOW, do you know what this glass is doing here?'
SCO (By this time totally incredulous):	'I rather think, Supply Officer, that it was left here by someone who didn't take it away.'

Later in the watch, the Cox'n was seen to remove the offending article behind his back.

SCO:	'Who's that whistling in the Control Room?'
No reply.	
SCO:	'Find out who it was and make them stop immediately Cox'n.'
Cox'n:	'Right away, Sir.' Fighting hard not to blush.

Overheard in the Food Re-hydration Centre:

Mac:	'I want to get off this thing as soon as it surfaces.'
NAVO:	'Hope you can walk on water.'
Mac	'No sweat, I'll borrow the XO's sandals.'

for years I've been working in my lab perfecting the formula | Yes, by only taking four of these special pills a day, illness has | mankind knows it will be banished, sickness will be a thing of the.. | past.... unfortunately there's been one or two unforeseen marketing problems.

The Scene: Submarine at 250ft, mid-afternoon in the Junior Rate's Dining Hall. Lots of heads stuck in Part Three books, while in the fore-ends, the rams are being exercised:

MEM R: 'Gosh, where did that air come from?'

RO.R: 'That's all right, they've just opened the main access.'

MEM R: 'Oh, that's ok then.'

Overheard in the Control Room:

CCWEA C: 'The submarine must weigh a set weight when dived otherwise we would sink.'

MEM G: 'We usually do with the XO's trim, don't we?'

Moving back to the Control Room:

SO   'I've just been back to Manoeuvring. It's quite nice back there, lots of pretty dials and things!'

EOP actions for HP gas burst, MC patrol:

1.   SWITCH ALL MC FANS TO FAST SPEED.

2.   ACT AS MESSENGER BETWEEN IMP/LANUCHER SUPERVISOR OR IMP/DCHQ AS REQUIRED.

3.   FETCH CHARGE CHIEF'S SHOES AND SPECTACLES FROM BUNK 122.

Chief Doc, mumbling to himself on Two Deck,

"Bloody typical, if they can't pick it up on Sonar, then it doesn't fucking exist."
Who are they?
What doesn't exist?

`KEEP PUMPING FROM M's....`

TICKED OFF?

Quas reckons that the best way to count off the days on patrol, is to just count the Sundays. It sounds less, he says O.K. Quas,

FUCKIN' THREE!

WHAT WAS SAID ABOUT THE LAST 'REVIEW'

The letters were nice, now all they need to do is get them in the right order.....
Education Officer.
. . . .
Bloody typical, five copies in each mess, and we can't even get boiler water chemistry chits xeroxed.
Chief Tiff.
ED., good point Al, and boiler chem. chits normally get more laughs too.
. . . .
Not too bad for a first attempt, but not enough tits.
DMEO
ED., In an attempt to rectify this problem sir, we're including an article about the Nav centre this week.
. . . .
Brilliant. bitingly funny. Tellingly witty. Trendy. A Master-piece. By far the most outstanding example of underwater literature I ever read
JOE B.
ED., Aw shucks.

QUOTE OF THE WEEK

"I think I'll get up in the morning, and do chemistry"
P. Crawford. M.D.

Overheard in the Control Room:

LWtr F:	'Steve, have you got your docs back from the Captain's inspection yet?'
PO(TS):	'No, he can't have done them all already.'
LWtr F:	'Why not? What else does he have to do?!'

Overheard in the fore-ends:

LH G:	'What's the difference between the Fwd and Aft escape towers?'
MEM T:	'About 400ft!'

Scene: WT Office, LT McL doing his Part Three.

RO C:	'Sir, are you going to be an OOW?'
LT McL:	'Yes, eventually, why?'
RO C:	'I hope you're going to be better than this CRAP on here!'

LT B (the undergraduate) to Steward S:

'Can I have an omelette, plain, with cheese and mushroom in it?'

The scene is the Control Room during fast cruise at Faslane and the new XO is desirous of substituting on the periscope two officers for chiefs, 'No-Legs' M and B.J.:

Captain:	'Leave them there. They're very experienced senior rates. Besides, they're the only ones who can see under the fog.'

Why does LT W keep asking the new MO to give him an enema?

The doctor innocently asks a steward at breakfast for a small round of toast. The leading steward supplies the delicacy as ordered, one inch in diameter (with crinkly edges).

'Not the kind of thing to do on a Sunday,' pouted Daktari (the doctor).

The leading steward obviously is a man who will need watching.

THE CREW

All at sea on HMS *Repulse* (continued):

The scene is the Control Room. Hydrogen gas is being added to the loop. SO is OOW. He notices that the skipper is smoking a cigarette:

Supply Officer: 'Excuse me, sir, do you mind not smoking as hydrogen is being added to the loop?'

Captain: '**** me!' (Or words to that effect.) Hides fag.

In the absence of a medical officer on a submarine, the 1st Lt takes over this role, can you believe that? The 1st Lts I have known in twenty-two years in submarines would not make the crew happy having him poke and prod them.

Ask any Jimmy 'what is sugar diabetes?' and the answer you will get is 'a Welsh flyweight.'

Ask any Jimmy 'what is a mastectomy?', and the answer you will get is 'a sailing ship going into dock to have its rigging removed.'

Fills you with confidence, eh?

It is night-time and the boat is at sea, heading towards the patrol area. AB O visits the captain's cabin to advise the illustrious occupant of a contact. This done he departs, drawing the curtain which flicks on the white lighting.

BEEP, BEEP, BEEP, BEEP.

'SCOOW'

Captain	'Send AB O to my cabin.'
Captain	'You turned on my light when you left.'
AB O	'No I didn't, sir.'

AB O beats a retreat and draws the curtain, once more throwing the cabin into white lighting.

The skipper's comments are not recorded, but for one commanding officer it looks like being a ****ing long patrol.

WEA2 T (Part III and Bar) was heard saying:

'I ain't going in the ******** fin. I'm a senior rate.'

BLEEDIN' TIFF

```
S.O. " My next job will be in charge of a desk"
N.O. " Yes,you don't have to TRIM a desk Do You"


Heard in the NAV CENTRE
WEM Smith(with trousers undone)
"Do you want to look down here NAV CHIEF"

Heard in Control Room

S/Lt Hopwood " We've got an epic movie this week
                  It lasts for 1hour and 60 minutes"


I have a "friend" who is a constant dieter.
One day after bemoaning his lack of success
he asked a young STWD
" What would you rather have, a skinny irritable
  PWEO, or a fat jolly one"            .
STWD " Just how fat do you have to get to be jolly"


PWEO's explanation of SUFFICIENT and ENOUGH.
"When the STWD's cut me a piece of cake I get SUFFICIENT,
 WHEN I cut a piece of cake I get ENOUGH!!!"


GEDGE "I've just got ridof all the shitfrom the
       Ballast Space"
John Main " Yeah, you came out!"


             ODE TO PWEO

          MY BODY KEEPS ADJUSTING
          UNDER MIDDLE AGE ATTACK
          MY WAISTLINE"S PUSHING FORWARD
          WHILE MY HAIRLINE'S FALLING BACK
```

A certain frog-faced LWEM is thinking of signing-on so that he can, and I quote:

'Walk around with my hands in my pockets, have every afternoon off, have cocktails during the dinner hour and go drinking with Phil White and the CRS – just like my navy chief.'

Well done, Froggy, the navy needs men like you.

Seaman G looms in the sick-bay door and wails:

'I've just been sick. Have you got anything for it?'

The LMA, with characteristic sympathy, hands him a bowl.

S-class submarine alongside in Faslane. We had the pleasure of the Queens 1st Foot and Mouth, or some regiment close to that name, on board. These were all in No.1 uniform, which made us look very rough indeed, and we were in posh No.8s.

As the afternoon progressed, the trot sentry was confronted by a very smart sergeant on the casing, who wished to speak to the 'corporal of the Horse', soonest. The trot sentry, thinking this 'corporal' was the same rate as a leading hand – wrongly, he was a warrant officer – made the following pipe, 'Corporal of the horse, gangway at the gallop.'

Much merriment 'tween decks, except among our khaki-clad comrades.

It was said in the Control Room that the best the NAVO could muster when asked by the captain where we were was, 'At sea, Sir.'

Bong heard in the MC – situation, looking at a 1983 calendar:

SW 'I see there's one Friday the thirteenth this year – in June.'
YW 'Is there? Whereabouts in June?'

The boat is in anti-Jezebel routine:

A voice: 'What do we do if we find Jezebel?'
Doctor (in a visible state of frustration): 'Draw lots for her.'

A SAILMAKERS GUIDE TO BIG (AND WE MEAN BIG) STITCHES.

Overheard . . . . .
Scouse "I'ts like Coronation Street back aft at the moment."
Tony H "Yeah, especially with Hilda Hutchinson."

Now steady, young Tony, what with Shagger(stitch) hearing you call him a
"loud mouthed, big headed oaf¥ your time in submarines could already be coming
to an end.   "

Chas Foy was heard to say, while standing in the scran line one day after a
bollocking from DMEO (whoever that is):-
    "DMEO's one redeeming factor in his favour is that he's only got one bad head
whereas Ted's got loads."

THE 1ST ? LT. (it has been said)

The Jimmy brings a picture of his wife to sea so that he can remember what she looks like.. .... Oh really......Dear Mrs McClement,	The Jimmy says he does not read pornographic literature, he just looks at the pictures......?
(can he remember when he proposed to you? ....these rugby fanatics go to lots of drunken house parties, you know.)	When asked about his brother, The 1st Lt. said " Yes, he is senior to me, he's a Lt Cdr." Then with a look of amazement and discovery in his eyes, looks down at his shoulder an exclaims "Oh, goodness, I'm a Lt Cdr as well." The mind boggles.

A SMALL CORNER
(in memory of Scouse Cogley)

DMEO..."MMS-MAN. Testing communications,

       how do you hear me."

COGLEY "Loud and clear, how me?"

DMEO..."Loud, but distorted."

COGLEY "Say again?2

AND

COGLEY "T.G. Main Machinery, open your bilge
        suction."

SPLASH "Say again."

COGLEY "T.G. what did you say?"

SPLASH "I said, say again your last."

COGLEY "Roger."....... Silence.

AND ANOTHER SINBAD MASTERPIECE

COGLEY "Man.Rm.-MMS, finnished
        transfering to MUF, 450 gal.
        transfered, lined up to
        transfer from 2 made water
        to top up 2 reserve."
MAN.RM. " Roger 450gal. transfered
        to MUF, leave the transfer
        to 2 reserve and come to
        manoeuvering and brin the
        tank state board up to date
        for night rounds."
COGLEY "Roger, transfering now."

Continuing trials and tribulations of being MO on an SSBN:

Sickbay telephone: Beep, beep (or noise to that effect).
MO: 'Apothecaries' Hostel, medical officer speaking.'
CO: 'Captain, can you come and see me?'
MO: 'Oh, umm, er, yes, Sir.' (blush, fart, etc.)

Overheard in the Control Room:

Main Broadcast: 'DO YOU HEAR THERE, THE REACTOR IS CRITICAL.'
O/S H: 'God, that sounds serious.'

O/S B (to the navigator): 'Sir, I hear you are the next XO of Unseen.'

NAVI: 'Yes.'

NAVI departs from the control room.

O/S B:' 'I know what ******* draft I'll not be putting in for now.'

AB B was heard to say, prior to his firefighting board:

'If he doesn't ask me everything to do with firefighting I'll smash his face in.'

AB S: 'The TASO is looking a bit chunky these days, maybe his next draft will be as a WEO.'

The same AB S: 'I wonder when CPO C last had sex?'

AB N: 'Whenever it was it was probably with a bloke because there is no chance of him trapping a woman!'

S/LT H talking to Manoeuvring: 'After the evaps are shut down are they going aft?'

And again AB S: 'How come you're allowed to wear those shoes in the Control Room.'

LWtr: 'Well, as I was going to be an officer, in fact I am almost one now, I can wear what the **** I like in the Control Room.'

Heard after a somewhat heated discussion about whether the OOW or OPSO is more important. After the OOD was gone:

POTS. 'Where does that PRAT get off?'

OOD (still being in earshot): 'Faslane, isn't that your stop?'

During rounds of One Deck:

TS 1: 'The Cox'n has lost loads of weight, yeah?'

AB N: 'I don't really take any notice of the Cox'n, that is unless he is swallowing the vices set on Ship Control.'

Overheard in the Control Room:

POCK talking to the WEO: 'Yes Sir, you may as well go back to bed, nothing's happening.'
As the WEO walks away POCK is heard to say (under his breath): 'Stops you blocking the
passageway you fat git.'

PO W said that JD looks sexy with long hair.
(Nothing wrong with this man, Editor.)

AB T said that he is going to give a lecture on sleeping; in fact, the CO can do it:
he gets more rack time than anyone.

Legend tells of an old A boat returning from foreign parts, on which one of the
crew had smuggled a monkey on board for a bet when he was confused with
the ale. However, news of the extra rating reached the Bun House once the
boat sailed, and the skipper decided to have a locker search in order to find the
said stowaway.

The Wardroom were worried that the crew might catch something nasty
from the monkey...it was more likely the monkey would get something nasty
from the crew!

It was obvious that the monkey would have to be drafted ASAP...so he would
leave via the Fwd SSE.

Bets on his survival went like this as the boat was at 200ft:

20/1	Against his getting to the surface intact.
15/2	Would he be able to clear his ears as he would be going up at 20ft/second.
25/1	Could he blow out all the way to the surface, as he had been told to do???
50/1	His Fez would come off on the way up.
100/1	Against his getting 'Survivor's Leave' if he made it, and any submarine pay due.

Even money the rating who brought him on board would be found and
punished.

As was said afterwards, who will be missed most – submariners or monkeys?
Any bets on that one?!

'Boy it's great being back at sea... the cry of the gull.....

.... the throb of the powerful engines..... the lilt of the deck......

--- the smell of the diesel----- bacon and eggs ..the crash of the waves...

------ Hugheeeee

B I L L Y   D I T

```
Early morning, two o'clock - there is a nasty swell.
The planesmen are both working hard and doing pretty well.
Of course, we've got the first team on, with Seth and Bear and Bill,
So anyone to follow that will find it all uphill.
The ordered depth is 65 and so to that we keep -
We've all been at it for an hour and only gone 3 deep!
Now, from back aft we hear the cry 'The extraction pump is broke!'
And working on it whilst at sea is really not at all a joke -
So when a certain RPO (I think they call him Brian -
Got a beard, wears glasses and, you know, he's always cryin')
Decides to slur the forward staff, it isn't very nice,
So I was summoned to back aft and now he pays the price.
"There's no way that I'll fix this pump while all you wankers forward
Are trying to play at aerodynamics..." (His statement was quite HORRID!)
And so to NEO we'll say "Send Brian up to 'plane,
And if he goes off depth at all, he'll really feel the pain
Of Seth and Bear and Bill and all - we'll really give him hell,
'Cos planing isn't easy when there's twenty foot of swell!
```

* * * * * * * * * *

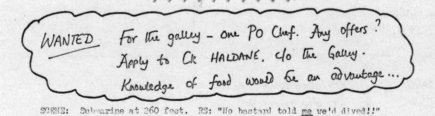

WANTED For the galley - one PO Chef. Any offers? Apply to Ck HALDANE. c/o the Galley. Knowledge of food would be an advantage...

```
SCENE:  Submarine at 260 feet. RS: "No bastard told me we'd dived!!"
```

Before we embark on the next few stories, a few words of explanation, particularly for those of you not quite familiar with the vagaries of submarine directional and pitch control. The rudder enables the submarine to point itself in the chosen direction. The aft and fore planes are essentially horizontal rudders that control the submarine's depth and pitch. Imagine trying to control a 400ft-long, 15,000-ton metal tube underwater using two little sticky-out wings. The whole evolution is made more difficult by the Ship Control Officer of the Watch Scow, whose sole aim in life is to pump water in and out of the submarines as quickly as possible, making it challenging, if not impossible, for the planesmen to keep the submarine on depth or an even keel. Now read on...

PWEO AS SCOOW: 'How's the trim?'
AFT PLANES: 'We're on course, Sir.'

PWEO AS SCOOW: 'This is a quiet watch!'
AFT PLANES: 'You should be sat here.'

FORE PLANES: 'Why do you call the PWEO chip pan?'
AFT PLANES: 'Cause he is so easy to flash.'

PWEO AS SCOOW: 'I keep twenty times more watches than the other SCOOWs.'
AFT PLANES: 'No you don't sir, it just seems that way when you're sat here.'

SCOOW: 'How's the trim?'
Foreplanes: 'Like "Spot the Ball", million to one chance of getting it right!'

Who said?:

'The MEO's got a zit right in the middle of his forehead that makes him look like an Indian?'

IS THERE HOPE!

TASO: 'How often do we do Reactor DAILY Safety tests then?'
OS B: 'Err...once a week, Sir!'

AB N: 'The reason I have a fat *rse is because I had hayfever when I was younger.'

Bloody Hell!!! Editor.

The POSA to nobody in particular:

'They reckon when you make love its equivalent to running 5 miles. I reckon in the past twenty-one years I've covered 2.5 miles – and most of that on my own!'

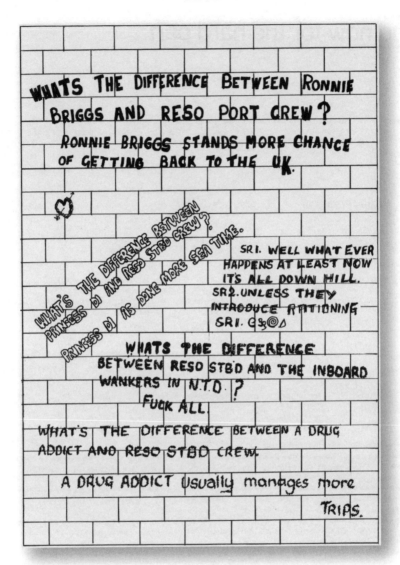

Overheard in the laundry:

'It's unusual for the chief stoker to be accused of sexual harassment, at least by a fellow human being.'

Scene: S-class submarine on the way down to Guz from Faslane, on the surface. As it was a nice day, a dozen or so of us were catching a few rays on the casing prior to diving stations. We were informed by the OOD, that a RAF Nimrod

And now for the hard part

EDITORIAL

Well, despite all advice, here's another rivetting, morale boosting issue of the Review - its made a happy man very old !! Its a bad state of affairs when Terry Waite's due home before we are.

CLASSIFIED ADS

For sale   170 Pewter Tankards - inscription may need alteration. Contact Canteen Manager (Stbd crew).

Wanted   Female lead vocalist for up and coming Rock Band. Must sing like Elkie Brocks, look like Felicity Kendal and drive a mud splattered Lambourghini with a crate of Blackthorn in the boot. - part 3 qual an advantage. cointact Ch Doc 235.

Items Wanted - Midget, Trampoline, Whip, Donkey. No weirdos
              please!!   Contact Willie - 241

Wanted   Blue buttons - contact Smudge - 3 deck.

Wanted   8's sleeves - contact Knocker - 3 deck.

****
Is it true that during the treasure hunt the SCO ws looking for the ba-
llast pump in AMS 1???
****
Apparantly Tam (flat back) Hutton cant get to sleep for the noise coming
from Magnus's pit.
****
During another exciting watch in Manouvering room the topic of convesa-
tion was blood pressure.
R.P.: "Did you know that the giraffe has the highest blood pressure of
any mammal? So the blood can reach it's brain !"
Big Mo : "In that case Lt Law's blood pressure should be higher than
mine!"
Lt Law : "WHO SAY'S THE BLOOD GETS TO MY BRAIN ??? "
****

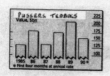

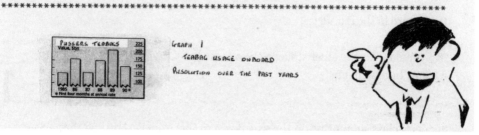

GRAPH 1
TEABAG USAGE ONBOARD
RESOLUTION OVER THE PAST YEARS

would be flying over us, and wanted to take a few shots of the boat (foolish man). 'Stand by for the flyover,' came the pipe.

A few moments later over came the Nimrod, flying low. Without a word being said the assembled rabble turned about, dropped strides, and mooned. The pilot must have been a good S.O.B. as he came round for a second run. For this, we assumed the position and, as one, saluted.

When we got the photographs on the boat the skipper remarked, 'That's the cleanest I've ever seen you lot, and how come I can't get you in a straight line like that on divisions, eh?'

You can't help but wonder what the 'Crabfats' thought of a Nuclear Strikeforce Submarine when they saw the snaps...

Overheard in the forends:

LMEM McG   'Sleeping between two tiffs is a real pain in the arse.'

Q 'How can you tell if the leading cook has looked in the mirror?'
A 'His footprints are on the sink.'

BONG from the present (HMS *Repulse* Part Three):

XO:	'What is the minimum depth of an Mk24 torpedo?'
JS D:	'50ft, to avoid surface capture.'
XO:	Very good. What is surface capture?'
JS D:	'Ermm, if we put it above 50ft the Russians can get it, take it back, and strip it down.'

'What will the new Cox'n be like?'
    'Tough. The sort that eats sardines without bothering to open the tin!'

Chapter Two

ENTERTAINMENT

MORE TIPS ON HOW TO BE A SUBMARINER:

- Sleep on the shelf in your wardrobe. Replace the wardrobe door with a curtain. 2 to 3 hours after you fall asleep, have your wife whip open the curtain, shine a flashlight in your eyes and shout, 'Sorry mate, wrong rack.' For added realism, get your wife to repeat this 10 minutes later.

- Renovate your bathroom. Build a wall across the middle of your bath and move the showerhead down to chest level. Shower once a week. When using the shower turn it on, step in, get wet, turn it off, get out, stand in the hall, soap up, get back in, turn on the shower, rinse off. Use no more than one gallon of water per shower. Get dry using a small, dirty hand towel.

- Take hourly readings on your electric and water meter. For added authenticity, report these to your wife. For even more, get your wife to question every second reading and demand you repeat it.

- Invite guests to your house, but don't have enough food for them.

- Wake up every night at midnight and have a peanut butter sandwich on stale bread. (Alternative options: cold beans and cornflakes, canned ravioli or soup.)

Keeping the crew entertained during long periods at sea is a major evolution in itself. The navy has done its bit by imposing the six-on, six-off watch system which leaves little time for anything other than eating and sleeping. But in the odd hour or two the submariner finds that he has for himself, he can participate in a variety of pleasurable pastimes; the Submariners' Sods Operas, some of which rival West End shows in their staging and content; the ship's quiz; film nights; game nights; pub nights and the ubiquitous Uckkers Championships.

'is,2 that bastard'

DID YOU FLUSH?

REMEMBER: LHOM IS WATCHING

YOU !!

ENTERTAINMENT

FROM THE ENTS O.

Now that Christmas is over time for some serious entertainments! The Sports Quiz is starting on Monday 30th December and will run every monday beginning at 16.45 in the JRDH. The first round is a straight knockout competition. All welcome to support or have a laugh. I'm still looking for teams for the General Knowledge Quiz and the Give Us A Clue. These will also run during the Dogs on dates to be arranged. I need more than three or four teams in each to make a decent competition so names to me ASAP. The next Movie Matinee will be on Sunday 5th January and is Naked Gun 2½. Whole Ship entertainments begin with the Pub Night on New Year's Eve with music for every one to sing along to. Casino Night will be on Wednesday 15th January. I need volunteers to man the tables. So anyone willing to do this names to me.

Keep the dits for the magazine coming in. Stich up your oppo as often as you like. No more about the Pusser as I already have enough to last the whole patrol !

dog and duck

BINGO

NEW YEAR'S EVE THEME PARTY

COME AS YOU WERE WHEN THE NWI TEAM ARRIVED

DRESS OPTIONAL

COMMENCES 2045 TIL CAPTAIN'S TABLE

ENTRANCE FEE - VARIOUS IN AID OF
JEANIE DEANS PEGASUS BED APPEAL

FOOD   CELEBRITY GUESTS   SURPRISE GUESTS

KARAOKE   SPECIAL GUESTS   FOOD

SLOP O' KEEPS THE TRIM.....

PLEASE SIR, CAN WE PUMP FROM 'M'NO1 PLEASE!

Uckkers is the naval equivalent of Ludo, but it is a lot more intricate. To give readers some idea of the complexity of the game, if Stephen Hawking played a board game he would play Uckkers.

Spectators watched open-mouthed as an ever youthful Joe B. steered the Moonies to a surprise five-point victory over the much-fancied Ballbusters. The Moonies glib and sure-footed tactics left little room for the XO and Cox'n to lend their weight to the attack, and it was only in the closing moments of the game that the leading writer produced the daily orders book and asked the Jimmy to sign it. This threw the Jimmy ten left, he answered Cock Robin which was wrong, but the Quizmaster wavered saying, 'Well, it's from the same book,' and promptly gave him ten points.

After the match there was a heated argument, as the Cox'n accused the Moonies of drug-taking, which only turned out to be religious fervour. When asked for his comments, the XO told our reporter to 'Bog off and get a flaming 'aircut.'

In view of this unexpected defeat, the Primary Samplers have increased their already punishing training schedule. Mid-question star Paul Astley is now one in four and it is believed that the Chief Doc only left his bunk once last week, and then only to change his copy of the *Encyclopaedia Britannica*.

Just a quick one, remembering the days of the three-reeler movies, we (*Sceptre*) had been designated a movie officer (wow!). This was to prevent all of the bitterness and mud slinging between messes. The movie officer was a Sub Lt, SJO we called him, silly jobs officer. You know the type, keen as mustard and as thick as mince. Prior to sailing on patrol, the SJO went to collect the movies, loaded them into the tilley and brought them down to the boat. The duty watch duly stowed them – twenty-five cans.

Nothing was shown during passage routine, with fire, flood and famine exercises. Once dived, the movie list went up outside the Cox'n's office on two deck. It was divided into three columns; wardroom, senior rates' mess and junior rates' mess. The movies to be watched by each mess were noted underneath, so there could be no complaints.

The first to be watched in our mess (SRs) was *Run Silent Run Deep* with Burt Lancaster et al. So, once we had rewound it, it was flashed up – *Noddy and The Kite*! I went to the Bun House to see SJO and the place was in uproar. The movie they should have had was *Hamlet*; what they got was *Gulliver's Travels* (in colour). The JRs had faired no better, instead of *Dirty Harry* they got *Son of Sinbad*.

Out of the twenty-five cans, we had six John Wayne films, *The Eiger Sanction* (in English and German) and *Ring of Bright Water*. On that patrol we had John Wayne in the Mess. I was treating people with snow blindness, altitude sickness and frostbite following *The Eiger Sanction*. After *Ring of Bright Water*, we had hard pad, mange and Otterdick. (Otterdick?! Med. in conf.)

It transpired that when SJO had gone to collect the films he had been very abrupt with the movie manager, demanding to be seen first as he was an officer. The leading hand was most helpful following this discussion, went and packed the movies for SJO, sticking to the list he had been given. He even put them in the cans and carried them to the submarine's transport. (Revenge is sweet.)

That patrol went slower than any I can remember. When we came back alongside, we rewound all the movies, upside down, put every one in a different can and changed the names on the reels. We were told they were going to a Bomber. I hope that the Bomber, officers and ratings who had the pleasure of trying to view these '*Sceptre* hybrids' realised the trouble we went through to produce them. SJO had an internal draft to wine manager. The movies were chosen and collected from then on by one SR and one JR. Otterdick was never a problem again. This was the only patrol I had been on without a Micky Duck. Fred Quimby was AWOL, not even a What's up Doc? Disaster, eh.

During long periods at sea the ship's quiz played an important part in on-board entertainment and provided an endless source of material for the ship's magazine. Over the years they have given rise to such golden nuggets as:

Q   'Who wrote *A Clockwork Orange?*'
A   'Eh...em...was it Max Jaffa?!'

Q   'Name the four seasons?'
A   'Salt, pepper, mustard and vinegar.'

Q   'What was Gandhi's first name?
A   Goosey, goosey?'

Q   'Johnny Weissmuller died on this day. Which jungle-swinging character clad only in a loincloth did he play?'
A   'Jesus?'

Q   'Name the funny men who once entertained kings and queens at court.'
A   'Lepers.'

Q   'What do you call someone who breeds silk worms?'
A   'A breeder?'
         Quizmaster: 'I'll open the question to the other team.'
         (Frantic buzzing)
AB S 'Sad?'

QUIZ

To win this weeks 'Special' prize just guess who STWD M'Gill was talking about:-

" you don't need much sleep, when you get to his age"

With a crew who's average age is measured in light years, we'll offer a few clues:-

1) The gentleman in question is an ex member of HMS Conqueror's ships company.

2) It's not the RS or the chief doc.

         Got it yet...... no ......well one last clue.

3) He's known affectionately to the rest of the crew as, the captain.

     Answers to the Editors by 12:30 Wedensday.

     Rules:- The editors decision is final.

The Captain and STWD McGill and all dependents are barred from entry.

     The editors decision is final.

PRIZES

     1ˢᵗ PLACE   'Great Escape' Video

     RUNNER UP ② 'Great Escape' Video's

S-class submarine at sea on patrol, the quiz was in its final stages. The Wardroom versus Junior Rates in the semi-final. (SRs waiting in the final.)

JRs question on history:

QUIZMASTER:	'Who was known as the hammer of the Scots?'
JRS:	'Stanley Mathews.'
QUIZMASTER:	'That question was on history, any further answers?'
JRS:	'Sorry, it must have been Nat Lofthouse.'
QUIZMASTER:	'I will give you a clue. He was Royalty.'
JRS:	'Oh, of course, Sir Bobby Charlton.'
QUIZMASTER:	'No points awarded on that question then.'

QUIZMASTER:	'What material did the Ancient Egyptians use as paper?'
PO B:	'Stone'
QUIZMASTER:	'Sorry, what did you say?'
PO B:	'Stone, I think?'
QUIZMASTER:	'I thought you did.'
PO B:	'It's not right then?'
QUIZMASTER:	'Give me a ******* break.'

Q	'What is the term for a squirrel's home?'
A	'Nuthouse.'

Q	'What is added to coffee to make Caribbean coffee?'
A	'Sand.'

QUIZMASTER:	'Which French Mediterranean town hosts a famous film festival each year?'
AB C:	'I don't know, I need a clue.'
QUIZMASTER:	'Okay, what do beans come in?'
AB C:	'Sacks?'
AB F (team-mate):	'You thick ******, it's Cannes you stupid bugger!'
AB C:	'Don't call me stupid, we loaded beans yesterday, in ******* sacks!'
QUIZMASTER:	'I think we'll move on, I'll not offer this one to the other team.'

QUIZMASTER:	'What is the capital of Italy?'
LS D:	'France.'
QUIZMASTER:	'France is another country. Try again.'
LS D:	'Oh, um, let me think, Benidorm.'
QUIZMASTER:	'Wrong, sorry, let's try another. In which country is the Parthenon?'
LS D:	'Sorry, I don't know. Geography's not my strongest subject.'
QUIZMASTER:	'I would never have guessed, just pick a country!'
LS D:	'Rome?'

Of all the quiz teams, none was greater or more feared than *Resolution*'s Primary Samplers, who were the chief doc and the three Primary Tiffs, highly intelligent and experienced nuclear engineers; well, nuclear fitters; well, they worn ovvies. They were the team to beat. In fact the opposition sometimes went to extraordinary lengths to knobble them.

On the evening of the semi-final against the Executive Bastards – a ruthless team whose members include the Cox'n and the 1st Lt – the chief doc was carrying out last-minute preparations in the Sick Bay. The doc was the quizmaster and had the somewhat helpful habit of leaving his questions and answers on his desk in the bay. The door burst open and in marched the Cox'n and the 1st Lt who promptly handcuffed the bewildered doc to the Sick Bay bunk, thereby, they hoped, securing a victory due to the Primary Tiffs not being able to field a full team.

The Primary Tiffs arrived at the Sick Bay and quickly assessed the situation. With typical resourcefulness they dismantled the bunk and the doc spent the whole quiz holding up the bunk he was still handcuffed to. The Cox'n stated he had a legal obligation to carry handcuffs and in this case the doc was showing signs of extreme agitation and hostility and clearly needed restraining.

Q   'What nationality is the Pope?'
A   'Is it Jewish?'

Q   'The terms curd and whey are associated with making what?'
A   'Would it be Milky Ways?'
TEAMMATE: 'For Christ's sake you're a bloody idiot, you should have known that!'

QUIZMASTER: 'Which is the largest Spanish-speaking country in the world?'
PO M: 'Barcelona.'
QUIZMASTER: 'I really need the name of a country.'
PO M: 'I'm sorry, I don't know the names of any countries in Spain.'

Q   'Who wrote the book *Chitty Chitty Bang Bang?*
A   'Clive Cussler.'

Q   'Which breed of goat do we get mohair from?'
A   'Labrador.'
QUIZMASTER: 'I'll open it up to the other team.'
A   'Hairy.'

Q   'Soilless agriculture is called what?'
A   'Mud.'

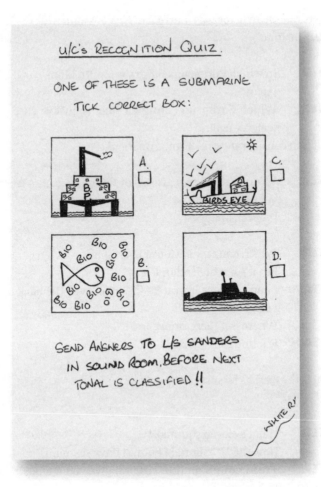

QUIZMASTER:	'Norma Jean Baker was famously known as whom?'
AB T:	'I know this, Elton John.'
QUIZMASTER:	'Eh, no, any answer from the other team?'
LS F:	'Billie Jean King.'
PO S (team captain):	'Oh ******* hell, I knew we should have played Smudge.'

QUIZMASTER:	'What happened in Dallas on 22 November 1963?'
LS D:	'I don't know, I wasn't watching it then.'

QUIZMASTER:	'In what year was President Kennedy assassinated?'
PO B:	'Erm...'
QUIZMASTER:	'Let's put it this way, he didn't see 1964.'
PO B	'1965?'

Q 'Which American actor was married to Nicole Kidman?'
A 'Busker Keaton.'

QUIZMASTER: 'In which European country is Mount Etna?'
LS C: 'Japan.'
QUIZMASTER: 'Which European country I said, so just in case you didn't hear, try again.'
LS C (after much consideration): 'Erm...America?'

QUIZMASTER: 'Arrange these two groups of letters to form a word – CHED and PIT.'
PO L: 'Um, Chedpit.'

QUIZMASTER: 'Which country is Mount Everest in?'
AB F: 'Err, it's not in Scotland, is it?'
TEAM CAPTAIN: 'I don't believe it, you ******* idiot, even the back afties know it's not in Scotland!'
AB F: 'Where is it then, smart arse?'
TEAM CAPTAIN: 'Err, um, er...' [blush]

Q 'What is the world's largest continent?'
A 'The Pacific'

QUIZMASTER: 'What's eleven squared?'
CPO B: 'How the **** should I know?! I'm a seaman!'
QUIZMASTER: 'True enough, in that case I'll give you a clue; it's two ones with a two in the middle.'
CPO B: 'Oh, must be five then.'

[The audience dissolved into fits of laughter and thereafter, when anybody met CPO B, he was greeted with 'Give me five.']

Q 'Name a film starring Bob Hoskins that is also the name of a famous painting by Leonardo da Vinci.'
A 'Err, *Who Framed Roger Rabbit?*'

QUIZMASTER: 'What was signed to bring the First World War to an end in 1918?'
LT D: 'Magna Carta?'
1ST LT (Team Captain): 'Oh my God.'

Q   'How many kings of England have been called Henry?'
A   'Err, well I know there was a Henry VIII, um...three?'

Q   'There are three states of matter; solid, liquid and what?'
A   'Jelly.'

QUIZMASTER: 'What is the name of the French-speaking Canadian state?'
LT A: 'Err, America? No, Portugal? Wait a minute, it's Canada? No, that's not right, you said state, Mexico? Oh **** me, Italy? B***ocks, Spain?'
1ST LT (Team Captain):   'Dear God, he's the bloody navigator!'

Q   'How long did the Six Day War between Israel and Egypt last?'
A   'This is a trick question. [After a long pause.] Fourteen days.'
TEAM MATE   'Yeah, very ****** tricky.'

Same Quiz a little later:

Q   'Where did the D-Day landings take place?'
A   [After a pause.] Pearl Harbour?'
TEAM CAPTAIN: 'Just stick to the ones on sport.'

Same quiz, even later:

Q   'Blackpool is a seaside resort on the coast of which sea?'
A   'English Channel, no, must be the North Sea.'
TEAM CAPTAIN: 'Don't you ever listen to me? Ignore his answer Doc (the quizmaster), he's a thick *******, I said just do sport!)

QUIZMASTER: 'What is the infamous *nom de crime* of Boston resident Albert DeSalvo?'
PO C: 'The what?'
QUIZMASTER: 'The crime name, for God's sake. Like Peter Sutcliffe was the Yorkshire Ripper.
PO C: 'Oh, of course, he was the Boston Ripper.'
QUIZMASTER: [Stunned silence.]

QUIZMASTER: 'Who was the black musician who played the trumpet?'
LWEM N: 'That's easy, it was Satchmo; I see seas of blue, red roses too...'
                 [A truly dreadful impression.]
QUIZMASTER: 'Wrong I'm afraid, it was Louis Armstrong.'
LWEM N: 'You what? You're on drugs ...******!'

[The quizmaster fined LWEM N five points for unruly behaviour.]

Another form of entertainment, although this was not its intended purpose, was the weekly family-gram. Primarily used on Polaris and latterly Trident submarines, it was a short note, normally comprising twenty words, but allowing forty words every four weeks, which was sent by the crew's families to the submarine base then transmitted to the submarine. All these 'letters' were monitored to ensure they contained no bad news or secret messages that might effect the recipient, but nevertheless they were eagerly anticipated and certainly helped pass the long weeks at sea.

The only time I remember it being tried out on the fleet boats was during the Falklands War. The families of the crew of HMS *Conqueror* were issued with one forty-word family-gram. Due to operational constraints, the messages had to be severely shortened. They transmitted every second word, which lead to some very remarkable messages.

The senders had to be quite creative and imaginative to pack the family news into such a short message. Some examples follow:

A Captain once told me he received a family-gram that read:
   'Good news, bad news. The good news is the RAC recovery service is brilliant.'

To announce the arrival of a baby boy:
   'Cushion arrived Friday, it has a tassel.'

The slightly more racy:
   '...sitting here full of moans, what I'd give to jump your bones.'

The heartfelt:
   'Oceans apart, day after day,
   The price a submariner's wife has to pay.
   No kind words, no smiles to exchange, no arms to hold you on a bad day.
   Just cold hearts oceans apart.'

The risqué:

   '... thirty bonks enclosed. Did the ocean move for you?'

Back to the quiz:

QUIZMASTER:	'What's the highest mountain in the UK?'
AB A:	'Dartmoor!'
LS F (Team Captain):	'Oh for Christ's sake, don't ask him any more questions Doc (the quizmaster).'
QUIZMASTER:	'I'm afraid that defeats the whole object of the exercise.'

Chapter Three

COURT AND SOCIAL

EVEN MORE TIPS ON HOW TO BE A SUBMARINER:

- Sit in your car for six hours each day with your hands on the wheel and the motor running, but don't go anywhere. Install 200 extra oil-temperature gauges. Log the readings on all gauges and indicators every thirty minutes. Report these to your wife.

- Tag out the steering wheel, accelerator, brake pedal, clutch and cigarette lighter when you change the oil in your car. Ensure all your neighbours have tagged out their cars if they are within 300ft of you.

- Buy all food in cardboard cases. For added realism, place them on corridor floors and cover them with hardboard so you can walk on them.

- Have your guests stand to attention every time you enter the room and make them state quite loudly, 'Attention in the Control Room' or 'Make way for the captain'.

- Practise taking a shower with two pints of water, using one piece of soap for every ten people.

- Work in six-hour cycles, sleeping only four hours at a time, to ensure that your body neither knows nor cares if it is day or night.

- Listen to your favourite CD six times a day for two weeks, and then play music that causes acute nausea until you are glad to get back to your favourite CD.

- Buy old beer barrels, cover them with a piece of old curtain and use them as dining room chairs.

- Stand on your roof once every four days for six hours in the winter and don't let anyone in your house.

- Spend three or four hours waxing your floors to perfection. Then, just before they dry, invite all the neighbours over to walk across them. Then do it again.

The secret diary of G.P. (Age 12½):

MONDAY (YUK)

I hate Mondays – my Dad's always farting and swearing – Oh, about my Dad. He's called Lilly Mac, he's really fat and ugly. He just sits around all day just picking his nose and hitting me, quite often he says 'Life's a ****', I don't know what a **** is yet but I think it's something funny. The other thing about my Dad is he doesn't work much, he just tells everyone what to do – he's weird.

All the houses in our street are a bit odd, ours is especially funny, it's long and black with no windows and shaped like a penis. Inside, the rooms are quite small which means when my dad farts it smells everywhere.

I've got a brother called Nick, he's really stupid, I mean dense, thick as ******* my dad says.

TUESDAY

Went to the shop today, the man who runs our shop is really strange, he's called Ned. Everybody calls Ned a ******, I don't know what a ****** is either although he does sell 3 different types of chocolate.

On the way home from the shop I met uncle Hamish, if you thought daddy was fat you should see uncle Hamish – he's disgusting. I saw him in the shower once – great rolls of fat falling off each other then he farted and the whole room shook. I think uncle Hamish is really rude.

WEDNESDAY

At school we call the teacher Navvie, he's bald as a peanut and quite old too, he seems to like my dad, they are always talking about sex. I found out what sex is last week, its all in a book I found at school. Oh, and the teacher keeps telling me about it. I think it must be interesting, especially if you are a grown-up.

I've really started to enjoy cleaning recently; my dad makes me scrub the floors all the time. It's fun, especially when daddy stands on Nick's fingers. Daddy hit Nick again today, some grey mush came out of his ears, someone said it might be his brains but daddy says he hasn't got any.

THURSDAY

Me and my friend Ralph were really sick today, the house just would not keep still and we threw up everywhere, at least mine went into a bucket, Ralph's was all over daddy. Daddy sent me to see the doctor, he's about 3ft tall, even I look down on him. Anyway, he gave me some medicine and said, 'Don't ever call me a stumpy little git again, nithead.'

FRIDAY

Nearly the weekend. Nick and I are going Christmas shopping this weekend, we are going to get daddy a mirror, he's broken all the rest and I want to get uncle Hamish some soap, either that or a cork to poke up his bum.

    Anyway, must go, bye for now G.P.

CRS Ms' description of PO T.H.:
'He's that little, fat, yellow PO.'

Junior Seaman D is admitted to RNH *Repulse*, with tonsillitis, a case of the old deep throats. The divisional system ever alive and well:
    Scouse says to the Doc: 'What's wrong with him?'

DOC:	'Tonsillitis.'
SCOUSE:	'But he's had his tonsils out.'
DOC:	'Oh, yes?' [Smiling.]
SCOUSE:	'Yeah, he's got a great big scar on his tummy, ain't he?'

Hours after a dummy missile exercise, the Impmen were draining down under the hatch spaces to the MC bilges. Inevitably, the bilge alarm went off and PWEO was observed running from IMP, screeching, 'Radiation alarm!'

A fore-ends White Rat reports that Wreckage C sleeps at Diving Stations – in Ossie Allsopp's favourite resting place.

WEM 'Chicken' R., a baby Navy Queen, has come a long way since joining the boat and wailing to a certain medical man, 'I'm too young to join the submarines.' [Sob, sob.] There's still room for improvement, however.

LEADER F:	'Are you a cherry boy?'
CHICKEN:	'No, I'm a Mod.'

Leading Stoker S. asks newly joined MEM T if he's seen the Chief Mech:

MEM T: 'I don't know. What does he look like?'
LEADING STOKER S: 'A ******* overgrown gorilla.'

DMEO launders his radiation film badge.

All at sea on HMS *Repulse* (continued):
It was during the operational readiness inspection that the marine engineering officer decided to take a stroll back aft. Who should he meet in the Manoeuvring Room but a certain 2-ringer known as 'Larry' who opined, 'The machines work, but the men don't.'

For his enlightenment, the following:
'A normal (?) working day for a non-duty watch was from 0800 until 1830, a total of 10.5 hours. If one was duty one dipped-in by starting work at 0800 the day of duty and securing at 1830 the following day, usually working through the night, a total of 34.5 hours. Since flashing-up we have kept watches, repaired, maintained and scrubbed-out ever since. So pray tell us, sir, if this isn't working, WHAT THE **** IS???'
(Back Aft Stoker, White Rat)

Standing in the queue for scran during a fast cruise on *Sceptre*, we had a new S/R petty officer, who had been drafted to the boat from Gens (bad move Drafty). As we approached the 'get your hot plate here section' this new PO called out to the POCK:
'Chef' [the leading cook and the POCK looked around to see if anyone else was in the galley]
Undaunted he went on:
'Chef, can I have a softly boiled egg?'
'Softly boiled egg!', the POCK screamed, 'Softly boiled ******* egg!'
The POCK had to be helped up from the deck; the white string had burst in his Steaming Bats.
'God give me two boll*cks, give this hat rack a raw egg, tell him to shove it up his ar** for a week, that's the nearest he is going to get to a softly boiled egg on this craft.'
From that day on the new PO was called Softly Boiled.
The exact quantity carried by the POCK in the testicular region was never verified.

The SCOOW was extolling the virtues of the Channel Tunnel:

SCOOW: '…and it will benefit tradesmen, tourism and local businesses, not to mention the general economy.'

AFTPLANES: 'Won't do much for the trainspotters, will it?'

MO: 'Do you have any trouble passing water?'

AB D: 'Well, I felt a bit dizzy coming over the Eskine Bridge this morning.'

BARBER: 'How would you like your ears?'

AB T: 'If you could just leave them on the side of my head.'

WRECKER: 'Sex is like full employment; a nice idea but never happening in my lifetime.'

AB S: 'Do you think Salman Rushdie is ex-directory?'

AB S: 'If you're a secret agent, how do you know when you run out of invisible ink?'

AB N: 'Why don't men get pregnant?'

DOC: 'Any biological process that involves giving up smoking or drinking for any longer than eight hours is a no no.'

CHIEF TIFF: 'I'm as fit as a fiddle and they can't do sit-ups either.'

Chief Stoker decided to carry out CSST evolutions in a *Miami Vice* theme; he changed rig for each exercise. He probably took it a bit too far when he said to CSST1:

'Does this say HP air burst to you?'

Control Room:

'OPS, Warner, no rackets, all bands.'

'Warner, OPS, er…your mast is down.'

'OPS, Warner…oh sh*t 'ere.' [Blush.]

During a Polaris patrol the boat's magazine was being sold to raise money for charity. The editors sold them from a stall in the junior rates' dining hall. They used the favoured method employed by newspaper vendors of old, yelling out totally incomprehensibly headlines to attract customers:

'El E O Snort em et buysmen em to.'

They flocked to them in their thousands, well, hundreds... well, six crew members. After buying the magazine they opened it, and there was the headline: 'El E O Snort em et buysmen em to.'

SPO put on a Jimi Hendrix cassette on the mess player:
'This is from his early period,' SPO informed the mess.
'What, before he died?' asked someone.

CHIEF DOC: 'Most medics don't smoke, primarily because we have access to much better drugs.'

CHIEF DOC: 'Its not naval policy to declare anybody brain dead on a submarine; it might jeopardise the mental status of the rest of the crew.'

Overheard at a mess dinner:
'When the Mess President said I was sitting next to the charming, witty, articulate and good-looking CPO B, I never realised there must be two of them.'

The TG Tiff had recently got married to an airhostess:
MESS MEMBER: 'So what attracted you to her, apart from the duty free?'

'If they banned mining, would it go underground?'
'He got karate and karaoke mixed-up and finished up killing twenty songs.'

When he was in DQs, he knotted sheets together and made a moped.

Overheard in JRs Dining Room:
'All these computer games, films and books on board and he gets more fun from playing with a cardboard tube and a hamster.'

1st Lt and Cox'n examining spilt food outside the galley:
COX'N: 'Don't worry, Sir, it's just the POCKs way of attracting customers.'

'I'm not saying he was a bad planesman, but they fitted airbags to the one-man control'.

Just rush in 20 toilet roll wrappers, and 15,000 sheets of Xerox paper, to our offices, and by return of post, we will send you your very own 'Womble' lok-alike' bendy Puppy.

'I heard the 1st Lt's dog has been worrying sheep. It's telling them the Iranians have nuclear weapons.'

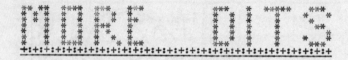

From the mouths of babes:-

Cogley "I won't believe we're goin 'ome until I hear it, in writin.*"
(Ed how very true, young'un, how very true.)

...and speaking of our very own, star MMS watchkeeper, we are endebted to
the 'grumpy corner' branch of his fan club for the following snippet:-

"While at HMS Raleigh, the Cogley bird and his class went on a trip to the
Natural History Museum in London. One of his classmates was heard to remark,
'keep moving Scouse, they're stock taking'."

It might not be considered, by some, the duty of the parish magazine to
make moral judgements but we feel we must bring to the attention of the
Squire the following quips:-
          (1) " Shut your flies, you're making my mouth water."
          (2) " Kiss me 'Hardie'."
          (3) " Do you want a dickin'."
In the interests of propriety we feel it better to conceal the identity of
the person involved; I mean, what would the clean shaven OA say if he
thought his opposite number was queer, ... or something.

Scene in the Senior Rates Mess:-
The RS, obviously thinking that the gathered mass could do with a little
cultural education, anounces.
"Right I'm going to play some classical music."
The tape we were treated to............. 'JIM HENDRIX'

Heard in the Junior Rates Mess:-
"I should have known it was 'blackwatch' cos all the SR's that are in
it are old c███'
No names, but he's an L/MA.
(Come and see me after school Glenda,   yours, Ch Doc.)

NCOW "Cogley you're looking miserable"
Scouse"Yeah, Am ferrup ana wanna gow ome, ana wanna see me mum."
NCOW "This is your home, lad. Look at the CERA in there, he's just like
       your mum, AND your dad."

Overheard in the JR's mess:
Nick Nichols "How will they be able to make soup when we run out of water, then."

....And finally Scouse said " awroyt, I know I do gob off a bit too much in our
mess, you could say I'm the Billy Budding of the JR's mess."

1st Lt in a reflective mood:

'We live on earth between heaven and hell and we need to understand both. This week I'm doing hell.'

'Men say, "I've got no kids, well none I'm aware of." You don't hear many women saying that.'

AB N, reading a magazine:

'I see the oldest man in the world is still alive.'

'I'm trying to get in touch with my feminine side. I've started burning the toast and driving badly.'

'How's Smudge, Doc?'

'Oh, he's holding his own.'

'Good, he must be feeling better then!'

LS F, in a boastful mood:

'I used to bonk twins. The lassie was all right, but I didn't fancy her brother.'

Overheard:

'Smudge watched *Titanic* – he was surprised when the ship sank at the end.'

Escape Locker Inspection; HMS *Sceptre*. Fwd Escape Compartment. Inspecting Officer from CSST:

Contents: One box of oxygen Draeger tubes.

One box of CO_2 Draeger tubes.

One box of CO Draeger tubes.

One tube of anti-sea sickness tablets.

One tin of assorted sweets.

One right-angled torch.

One box of forty-eight forget-me-not Durex.

INSPECTING OFFICER: 'In God's name Chief MA Why the Durex for Escape ?'

CHIEF MA: 'Well, Sir, you never know!'

S-class submarine at sea; the CPOMA is coming through the tunnel following the primary sample. He meets a young, wild-eyed, Part Three stoker:

STOKER: 'Did you hear the last pipe, Chief?'

Chief MA thinks, 'God, what have I missed?'

CHIEF MA: 'Go on Stokes, tell me.'

STOKER: 'They said that there was panic in the boat and the person responsible is to report to the Control Room.'

CHIEF MA: 'The pipe there was banging in the boat, you hat rack!'

Needless to say the young stoker was first on the list to have his ears flushed.

S-class submarine alongside in Devonport; shutdown. The Chief MA is in the main room with the EOOW, a warrant officer. On one of the panels in main room was a selection of dials which had been put in during build, these were of no use but proved a source of amusement when down the after hatch arrived two Sub-Lts. We decided to have a little fun, so the Chief MA rotated each dial and called out a number, which the EOOW noted down. It all looked very technical; there were seven dials in all. After a few moments one of the subs asked:

'What are you doing, Chief ?

'We are compensating for the peripheral loss in leakage flux, Sir,' the Chief MA replied. [This was rubbish.]

One sub said, 'Of course, of course. Carry on. Make sure you include the readings in Health Physics Report, won't you?'

Needless to say, no readings were ever disclosed.

S-class submarine at sea on patrol. The outside wrecker and the fwd SPO were in charge in the Laundry. The routine was to deposit your dirty No.8s in the Laundry and they will be on your bunk in the next two days.

The WEO, who shall remain nameless to protect his offspring, thought it would be a good idea to put a pair of his underpants in each pocket of his No.8s. Good idea? WRONG.

The fwd SPO found the offending 'kecks', which were white, of all colours! He rubbed the gussets of each with a Mars bar, then hung them on a coat hanger outside the Laundry with the following note pinned to them:

'Will the owner of these items of underwear please remove them before pestilence strikes the boat.'

A watch was kept on the offending items, and after three days the skipper took pity and had them removed by the W/D Room steward. The WEO never tried it again.

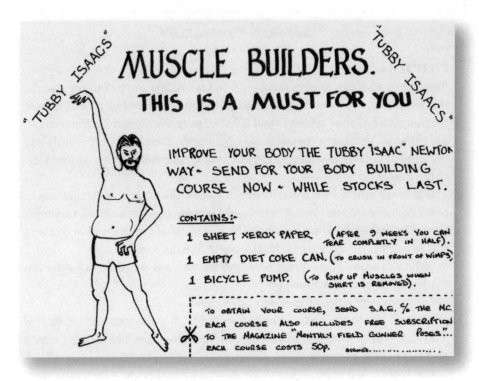

DO's interview re: 264s:

DO TO CHIEF MECH: 'I see that you are Roman Catholic, Chief.'

CHIEF MECH: 'Oh yes, Sir, born and reared as one.'

DO: 'Are you practising?'

CHIEF MECH: 'Oh no, Sir, I do it for real.'

S-class submarine at sea. Fire in the forends. The outside wrecker was in the canteen, on Fwd Escape. Lots of smoke; everybody in EBS; the Mars Bar machine was in meltdown. Wrecker collapses down the Fwd Escape ladder, close to croaking due to smoke inhalation. He was taken aft by the medical party and put on oxygen. After some time he comes to, takes off the oxygen mask, and says:

'Sh*t, that was close, I could murder a fag.'

'A fag?' the Chief MA said, 'my bum was making buttons thinking you were going to snuff it, and you want a fag? You will have to open the canteen, 'cos I've run out.'

SANDBAG THE SAILOR

CHAPTER ONE

'Hear ye oh knights, princes and kings, as I tell thee a story of many strange things; of beasts of the deep and monsters from hell and of a hero named Sandbag the Sailor, of whom I shall tell...' so sang the minstrel to the court of King Hamish the Heavy, the assembled dignitaries, their ladies and escorts and the guest of honour, Sandbag Sanders the Sailor, returned from his voyages with riches untold.

Our story starts in a waterfront bar called the Gimps in Belenshurgh. Sandbag had a ship on his slop chit, loaned by King Hamish and now needing a crew. Sandbag walked into the smoky bar-room, where the men were drinking and wenching. He ordered grog and turned to face the crowd.

'Who will sail with me on my next voyage?' shouted Sandbag, in a voice Ian Paisley would have been proud of.

The room went quiet, all eyes were on Sandbag.

'We will sail to strange and unknown lands, face hazards and uncharted waters. It will be a dangerous journey, but the rewards will be plenty. I have a ship and need of a crew.'

Sandbag looked around him at the men of Belenshurgh. Tough men, loyal men, they feared nothing. They were pissed, but they had heard of Sandbag and his past voyages. No one spoke.

'Okay, I'll cut the crap,' said Sandbag, 'we're going to find the *Golden Girder*.'

There were gasps of astonishment, eyes widened in fear and sphincter muscles quivered. No one seeking the *Golden Girder* had ever returned.

'Count me out,' came a voice.

'And me.'

'F**k right off.'

'Aww, come on lads,' said Sandbag, 'unlimited fags, all the gruel you can eat, and I promise I won't go ashore with the beer keys again.'

'I'll come with you, Sandbag,' came a voice.

'And what is your name, brave man?' Sandbag asked.

The man, Ralph, threw up noisily.

'Come then, Ralph, join me over here. Is there only one man in Belenshurgh brave enough to sail with me and Ralph?'

'Ralph and I,' corrected someone.

'You could make yourselves fortunes,' he said, 'come on, a few weeks away, no more nagging wife, no screaming kids and what's more, the price is right.'

'I'll go.'

'And me.'

'Argle, Eargle V'argle,' said George Peacock.

And so it went on until Sandbag had his crew.

'The provisions are aboard, the crew are ready, we're in plank state "A", she's ready to go,' reported Howling Mad Gilroy, Sandbag's second in command.

Howling Mad Gilroy was what was known, in layman's terms, as a bloody idiot. He had sailed with Sandbag before and was obviously stupid enough to do anything.

'Pipe harbour stations then,' said Sandbag.

The brow was removed, the ropes were let off and the telegraphs went to half ahead. The crowd on the jetty cheered and waved as the stokers shinned up the mast to rig the main engines. A pleasant wind and a fair tide were behind them as the *Spasmo 1* left Belenshurgh, perhaps to never return. The biggest cheer came from King Hamish; he still had the fag locker keys.

CHAPTER TWO

Two months out and the crew morale was low. The ship's cook, 'Salmonella' Spam Pohher, turned out the same old sh*t every day. The crew complained that it was sh*t for breakfast, sh*t for lunch and sh*t for supper – although the urinal cleaner was happy.

'Land ho!' came the voice of the crow's nest lookout. 'Starboard bow.'

A few crew tripped over him running to the ship's side. Sandbag looked at his charts.

'Bloody hell, George Michael is number one again,' he muttered.

They had come to the island called KA.

They went into a large natural harbour at the east of the island, where Sandbag took a small party ashore, leaving instructions to replenish the ship with water and collect any food and fresh fruit they could find and scrub two deck.

'I wonder if the *Golden Girder* is here,' thought Sandbag.

The *Golden Girder*, it was said, was a gift from the gods to A.G. BARR, warrior, philosopher and maker of Iron Bru. When Eruton fell to the marauding hordes of Wiggin, the Wigginers carried the *Golden Girder* away in their Triumph (Catsun hadn't cornered the market by then). However, with time, war, empires forged and fallen, the *Golden Girder* had been lost.

Sandbag was pulled out of his reverie by a loud roar and the screams of terrified men. He rushed toward the ship and beheld a sight that only few have ever lived to tell of. It was a giant, roughly man-shaped beast covered in hair apart from its knuckles which scraped on the floor. It wore what would become known as a boiler suit, white socks and civvy shoes, its most dominant feature a large protuberant eye in the middle of its forehead. Sandbag looked in his *Janes Book of Monsters* and was horrified at what he read.

'Cyclops Stig,' he muttered.

The Cyclops Stig was a creature that spent most of its time asleep, but, when awakened, it was a truly formidable adversary. It could crush a man, rip arms and legs from sockets and even eat someone whole. Its skin was tough and no arrow could puncture it, and its eye had 360° coverage. Its table manners were disgusting.

'Get back to the ship,' he shouted. (And when Sandbag shouted, everyone heard.) 'Back to the ship, quickly!'

He had read that the Cyclops Stig hated water and so would not chase them past the shoreline. They clambered into the boat and pushed off, but, unseen, the servant boy, Harry Cobbles, was eaten, which made a change from him eating someone else's scran. They got safely back to the ship and ate a hearty meal of Spam Pohher's speciality – sh*t, cold. Dusk, followed by darkness, fell over KA.

It was a pleasant night, marred only by the smell of the unwashed Cyclops and ugly Olliffe's dirty knicks, which even Stig wouldn't eat. Unnoticed, a lone swimmer slipped away from the ship and made his way toward the island. A few minutes later, a blood-curdling scream filled the night air. The crew were up instantly, like any highly trained body of men living by their wits.

'Over there!' someone shouted, as he saw the swimmer on his way back. The crew gathered at the port side to see Psyco Soapy Doy making his way back, with something in tow. As he came close they realised it was the Cyclops's head. They helped him up the side. Sandbag was there to greet him and bade Psyco tell of his adventure.

'I'm shy,' said Psyco.

'Come on,' roared the lads in unison.

'Well,' began Psyco, before he went on to explain how he had shaken the Cyclops with the DC lamp and then chopped off his head.

'Now that you have rid us of the foul Cyclops,' said Sandbag, noticing that the crew started yawning the moment he spoke, 'you may have anything you wish.'

Psyco whispered in his ear.

'Oh,' groaned Sandbag, 'okay.'

On returning from patrol, an S-class submarine tied up at Charlie Buoy overnight. (sunny, Guz.) It was decided to have a fancy dress night, but only gear from the Grade A rag-bag could be used. Failure to take part: fine one barrel of CSB. The evening went with a swing, with everyone taking part. There were gunfighters; highwayman; pirates; Indians; vicars; tarts; Elvises; Michael Jackson (alive then); the Incredible Hulk; Wee Willie Harris; Toulouse Lautrec. All were gathered in the S/Rs' mess, with the exception of one, who was usually first, when suddenly the mess door opened and in he waltzed.

From the neck to the deck he was covered in a pink sheet, held out from the body by a wire hoop inside. On his head he had an old-style ladies swimming hat, with a chin strap, worn back to front with two eye holes cut in it, this was pink as well. On the top of this he had glued a big, red, plastic lose, like those worn on Red Nose Day. The mess was in hysterics.

'What in nineteen navies have you come as?'

Wait for it...

'I've come as a boil,' was the reply.

Well, he was a back afty.

1

All buddies in boats, read on...

A Bomber out in the States after firing the Bird. The POMA, who will remain nameless but had a face like a camel sucking a Zube, had trapped a most beautiful thing scantily clad in black. Bragging in the Mess prior to meeting her that nothing could go wrong now, and he was off for two days of 'Heaven in a Motel'.

...However, three heavy back afties and the Cox'n handcuffed him to two barrels of CSB. He tried manfully to make the main access hatch, without success. Worse still, his lady love was trapped by the Chief RS. (Shame.)

As a young MA on a Bomber (off crew) we were asked to put names in a gash bin, anyone wanting a jolly to Malmo. (That's in Sweden, in case any wreckers read this.) Lo and behold my name came out. I was told to report to the cox'n for 'embarkation instructions.' So, reporting to the cox'n, I asked what my flight details were.

'Flight details, what flight details, here is a rail warrant to sunny Guz. When you get there report to the cox'n of HM/SM *Aeneas*, he will clue you up as to duties etc.'

'Duties etc.? Duties? I thought this was a ******* jolly.'

I am not saying she was old, but most of the crew had barnacle rash. We sailed the next day and my duties were lookout, wheel, telegraph and dogsbody. I thought I had the wheel mastered until, just prior to Malmo's outer areas, with the skipper on the scope, the orders went like this.

'Stbd 10.'

'10 of Stbd wheel on, Sir,' I replied.

(Mr Christian or what)

The skipper said, 'Ease to five.'

Now, I thought he said, east to five, so I said to the cox'n, 'which way's east?'

The Control Room collapsed in laughter. The skipper, with tears in his eyes, said, 'Have that put on Daily Orders, cox'n, I want the ship's company to know which ******* way is east!'

I managed to salvage some of my reputation when I solved the mysterious sickness on board. Dhoby [wash] the dishes in a different bucket to the one used to scrub the deck.

Moral to this story: never, but never, think a jolly means an easy time.

Chapter Four

WHO'S IN THE NEWS

STILL MORE TIPS ON HOW TO BE A SUBMARINER:

- Practise walking quickly with your back to the wall.

- Cut a twin mattress in half and enclose three sides of your bed. Add a roof that prevents you from sitting up (about 10in. is a good distance), then place it on a platform that is 4ft off the floor. Place a small dead animal under the bed to simulate the smell of your bunkmate's socks.

- Periodically shut off all power at the main circuit breaker and run around shouting 'fire, fire, fire.' Ensure this is timed to coincide with sleep time, and then restore power telling everyone they were 'crap' and would have died if it had been the real thing.

- Every four hours check all the fluid levels in your car and log the readings. Check the tyre pressure and replace air lost from excessive pressure checks. Be sure to place red tags on the ignition stating 'DANGER: Do Not Operate' while you perform these checks. Inform your neighbour as to placement of the red tags, the results of the checks, and have him repeat the checks because he did not see you perform them. Only carry out this routine late at night.

- Have the paperboy give you a haircut.

- Have your dinner guests work in two watches, each of six hours. Once they have settled into a routine, change the times around.

- Wash your laundry in a detergent that could be used as an insecticide or sheep dip. Make sure you lose at least one sock and one pair of underwear every other week.

● Run a tube from your car's exhaust pipe into your living room. Yell, 'Prepare to diesel!' and start the car. You must breathe the fumes for one hour.

SCENE ONE

Control Room, left-hand side. Enter CO after a bath and dhoby wearing Brut.

OPSO: Who's that brown hatter?

CO: 'Are you remarking about my after shave?'

OPSO (turning to CEP):   'Don't you dare drop your guts in the Control Room again.'

CEP: 'OUCH.'

SCENE TWO

Same place, four weeks later. Enter CO smoking the original Sir Walter 'bine.

OPSO: "Who the ****'s smoking camel shit in the Control Room?'

CO (from behind the OPSO's seat):   'Don't hit the CEP again CHOPS.'

We've all heard them at one time or another. Sitting in deadly silence and then a one-liner in a class of its own bursts forth from the mouth of some poor unsuspecting person. Here are a few collected over the past thee months:

N TO FP: 'Have you got any kids?'

FP TO N: 'No, I haven't.'

N TO FP: 'I've got a niece who's four!'

(During a conversation about a possible Channel Night.)

SW: 'Channel Night doesn't interest me, I don't drink when I'm duty'

T: 'I haven't got any half-blues anyway!'

(Whilst sitting in Manoeuvring.)

DP: 'In one month's time it's my dog's birthday.'

(SB walks into the Ship's Office.)

SB: 'I'm going to see the wife's niece tomorrow night, she's twenty.'

(Cheque Cashing queue before arrival in Rosyth.)

CC: 'Is this the queue for subsistence.' (Bless 'im.)

Once again our 'ALL SEEING'   Albino Rodent has come out of hibernation with yet another series of startling revelations that would set the whiskers quivering on even the blackest of black cats.......

"Most of this weeks Zaps concern, once again, members of Britians ' Elite Officer Corps, who like lambs to the slaughter, commit the gravest of mistakes in assuming that the White RAT ' Could'nt ' possibly have heard about this one"

Our first DIT concerns our everso hairy and bespectacled TWEO who, whilst idly chatting to the OPSO with the REA in attendance failed to notice the little pink nose sticking out of the fan trunking above his head and said....."HO.HO.. YOU KNOW SOMETIMES THE XO MAKES A MISTAKE AND CALLS ME THE ELECTRICAL OFFICER " says Eggers (under his breath) "THAT IS A FUCKIN MISTAKE "

Later the TWEO enters the Sound room and asks a startled CHOPS "WHAT HAVE YOU GOT FOR ME TO PLAY WITH ?" what further damning evidence can there be? especially with the search for the 'Voice' from our First issue still in progress.

Next.....the NAVIGATOR on the phone to Manoeuvring to his friend the DMEO... "IS YOURS STIFF YET ? 'COS EARLIER IT WAS ALL FLOPPY " ... of course he was Referring to the MEO's N.O.B.

And... SUPPLY OFFICER to the Control room at large "..PERSONALLY I SEE NOTHING WRONG WITH A LITTLE BLUSHER....."....KING HELL..

Also NAVIGATOR (again) to L.S. JONES..."YOURE GOING GREY L.S. JONES" came the reply "SO WOULD YOU IF YOU HAD TO KEEP WATCHES WITH WHAT I HAVE TO KEEP WATCHES WITH. OH DEAR.

Lastly...Our own desperate CAPTAIN has resorted to borrowing matchsticks from the NAV. CENTRE to try to keep a sombulant CPOSA awake on the after planes. And to think that we thought that SPIKE was Nodding in agreement to course changes... you'd get more joy from GEORGE...(THE MECHANICAL ONE I MEAN)

SEE YOU NEXT TIME BACKSTABBERS... BYE YAWL.

"HEY CH DOC I'VE JUST FOUND A CASE OF SAMONELLA ON BOARD"

"THANK FUCK, I'm REALLY GETTING PISSED OFF WITH THIS RED SHIT......."

Fred Layton says he knows fuck all about D.C.B and Lt SNOWBALL knows even less. Love telltale.

A Dit from DAVE LAWSON
I think a truck must have run over my HEAD when I was a kid...(don't we all Dave)

Conversation overheard in the senior rates annexe between SLINGER (ELTON) WOOD and GEORGE (YER CUNTeeee) HERRING......

SLINGER "Shot through on the training again, in your rack again I suppose"
GEORGE   "I was up yer C███"
SLINGER "You were up my FUCKING ARSE !" (SELF CONFESSED)
         Louis of Apoldo.

OUTSIDE THE W/R PANTRY
TASO "Don't you go to Church L/STD"
L/STD " Na I dont go in for this J.C. stuff, infact there only 2 people I believe in with those initials and thats JOAN COLLINS and JOHN CLEESE, i'm not supprised he aint come for a second comming as they hung the poor dude on his first arrival"
TSAO "they'll probably stick him in an electric chair this time"
STD WOOD " I think the PO CHEF is J.C. because he can feed 4000 on a couple of LOAFS and some FISH"

AB (Table salt) MOORE, at scran
Is it getting to that time of the patrol when certain ratings start to crack up and become very absent minded. Some very unusual things happen around this time, and this example must be one....
AB (Table salt) MOORE, while having scran, picks up the salt cellar unscrews the cap and pours salt all over his scran, looking up very puzzled he says aloud "SHIT WHAT DID I DO THAT FOR" as he scoops the salt off.
Conclusion Crackus upus dickus.........

JT: 'I've just bought a coat off the Coxswain!'
BB: 'Ere Ned, you live on this side of the world don't yer?' (Who knows what planet he's from?)

(A young stoker doing his joining routine in the ship's office.)
COX'N: 'Married or single?'
MEM A: 'I dunno!'

(Ship's office.)
S: 'I'm looking forward to getting home, the last time we came in the missus was expecting me and she had her sussies, stockings and a basque on.'
GI: 'A BASCCA!?' [Breathing Apparatus, Self-Contained Compressed Air.]

NS	'Are you busy?'
L WTR:	'No, I'm writing a book entitled *1001 Stupid Questions to ask Someone When They're Busy.*
NS:	'Oh, can you type this for us then?'

WATCH LEADER:	'Come left.'
SCOOW:	'Roger come left – starboard 15.'
F/PLANESMAN	'?????'

OS D:	'The new POCK wears cowboy boots, occasionally on the right foot.'

And from the same source:

'The POCK can distinguish twelve different types of cheese, just by reading the labels.'

XO:	'God gave me the priceless gift of being able to laugh at other people's misfortune.'

POTS:	'The Cox'n's started on-the-spot fines. I had to eat cream crackers with a glass of water on my head.'

OOW:	'How's the atmosphere, Doc?'
CHIEF DOC:	'I think we'll need a pointy stick and some holy water to sort it out, Sir.'

With just a wee while to go before we return home, it seems that a certain military atmosphere is starting to pervade the nooks and crannies of the boat. The lads, of all grades, are appearing with a variety of 'individual' coiffures. It is lunchtime in the J/R's dining hall and AB P makes a grand entrance with a haircut which could have been part of the Belsen joining routine. LMA (momentarily distracted from his scran):

LMA:	'I bet the Chief Ops has been involved in haircuts.'

(Pregnant silence.)

CHIEF OPS (at servery): 'It's wise to have an all round look before making such statements, Doc.'

(LMA blushes, general mirth ensues.)

Stwd K discussing the occupants of the wardroom:
   'There's an IQ of 180 in there, well, if you add them all up.'

From the same source:
   'If you put their heads together you'd make a plank.'

AME01:	'That article on Perishers makes the executive branch sound like super heroes.'
EPO:	'What does the skipper do all day then, Sir?'
AME0:	'SLEEP!'

During Operational Readiness Assessment the Sick Bay became (tut, tut) a Bunhouse Annexe, Captain SM10 being accommodated therein. The premier standing order in the Sick Bay is 'NO SMOKING' and was there not a fine to-do when the Great Man's ashtray disappeared on no less than two occasions?

A Board of Enquiry convened by the senior medical officer produced a pouting medical technician who flatly denied any conspiracy to prolong the captain's lifespan by discouraging him from smoking. It was also lies, he said, to suggest that he wore EBS in the Sick Bay whenever the captain succeeded in lighting-up the weed.

It was at about this time that Captain SM10 rounded on the doctor in the Bunhouse, saying (more or less along these lines) 'Your chief has hidden my ashtray on two occasions. If he wants to make an issue of it, HE'S PICKING A FIGHT WITH THE WRONG PERSON!'

Editor: Before Captain G departed he thanked the medical technician for his hospitality.

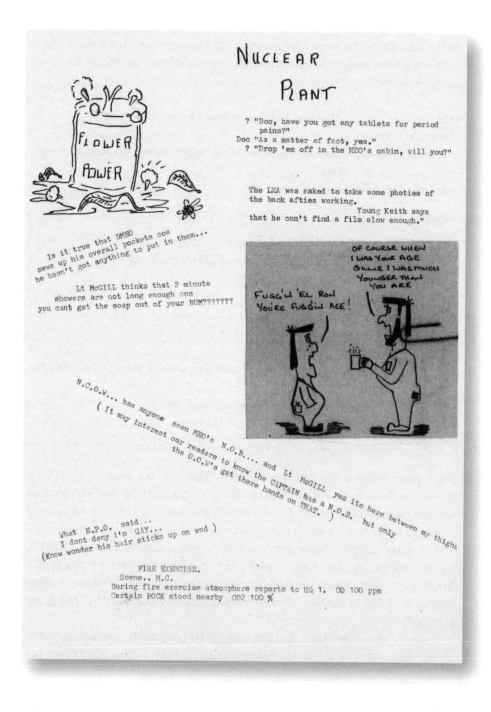

Junior Seaman D asked if he could get to the bridge by the main access hatch.

LT B was observed going on watch one hour early to relieve LT D on the bridge. Keenness? Or hadn't he been told that we had reverted to Zulu time?

The boat is alongside and LMEM F wishes to contact his mentor LT FB. He picks up the shore telephone in the Control Room and dials 222. A voice asks, 'Which service do you require?'

The scene is the Control Room during NWI. For exercise the boat (bows south) is about to be listed for missile jettison.

Main broadcast: 'Open 1, 2 and 3 starboard main vents.'

The captain enquires of the boat's angle.

'7° to port,' snivels the navigational supervisor.

The NWI team are not amused; the wrecker is in hysterics.

All at sea on HMS *Repulse* (continued):

Junior Seaman D is admitted to the Sick Bay on board for reasons which will be plain to all, i.e. the chief medical technician wished to evict Captain SM10 and thus stop smoking and also reduce his after planes watches. Anyway, chief ops is dutifully informed of the event. 'I don't see why the f**k he's turned-in, anyway, if he's not well enough to wield a whole Scotch-Brite, he can f****** turn-to with half of one.'

AB S:	'Do you practice safe sex?'
AB W:	'I've got a handrail round the bed.'

Heard at a routine drug-test interview:

LREG:	'Have you ever taken pot, LSD, crystal meth, crack, heroin, smack…?'
AB F:	'Not all at once!'

The chief mechanic (reactor tiff wise) on both *Sceptre* and *Turbulent* was known as Britain's worst dressed man, even in No.1s he would have to stand next to a skip full of rubbish to look semi-smart. A man who marched to the beat of his own drum and a great friend, I know he will not mind if I name him, so Yorky T, take two paces forward.

On *Turbulent* building in Barrow, he and I went into town to get him a new civvy suit. Yorky was dressed in a Grade A rag ensemble. On entering Burtons he asked for the manager. An elderly fellow came from the rear of the shop and, looking at Yorky, said, 'Can I help you, Sir?'

Yorky said, 'Yes, have you got a suit to fit me?'

To which the manager replied, 'If we have, some b******'s getting the sack.'

On the way out Yorky said, 'No problem Toby, I'll borrow one of yours, okay?'

DMEO to DANGEROUS in the Wardroom:

'I suppose you want me to eat Stwd McGill?'

'Not literally, Sir, I hope.'

At the end of Attack Teams:

XO: 'SLT H, I want you to do OPS next week.'

AB H: 'He might get some better solutions then.'

Overheard in the Sound Room:

AB G: 'I don't like going into the Control Room when the TASO's on watch. I'm scared I won't get past his relief that's growing on his nose.'

Overheard in the Forends:

MEM G: 'I knew I had seen LT R before. It was in Star Wars.' (The Bookie)

MEM R (talking about the PWEO): 'I think he wants to be like the WEO.'

LWEM C: 'What! Fat and ugly?'

CPO P TO WEM R: 'Why aren't you my relief?'

WEM R: 'Because I'm not big, fat and ugly.'

CPO P TO WEM R: 'Surely you don't mean CCPO F?'

WEM R (blushing and farting):   'Er, em, er, no I meant N W.'

Reading from the book *Resolution*:

And it came to pass that there arose, on board *Resolution*, a tribe known as the Ship Controllers, and they did wear brown shirts, much like those of the tribe of officers, and thus could you know them.

In the beginning, they were few in numbers, and scattered throughout the departments, but as the days of patrol grew longer, so their numbers multiplied, even though the Roy who was C did thrice refuse to join the tribe. So many did they become that the lieutenant who was first did take forth the supply officer, the guardian of the snorkers, and did place him in the watchbill of the officers of the watch, that they might be grown in numbers and go 1 in 5.

And yet still were the Ship Controllers so many in numbers that they did suffer the terrible plague of rack rejection, and they were named anew the Men with No Zs, and were doomed forever to wander the length and breadth of *Resolution* seeking for something to do, even into the end of patrol for so it is written.

Here endth today's lesson.

During Index LT B grabbed an EBS and, wearing it, rushed into the Control Room. Face turning an unhealthy shade of turquoise, he looked for an EBS coupling – only to find that no one else in the Control Room was wearing EBS.

Note to Part Threes: LT B doesn't listen to pipes.

2nd Sea Lords' team on an S-class submarine just back from patrol, riding in from Charlie Buoy. The news had been about the Royal Yacht, and the number of homosexuals on board:

'Of course, it's difficult to tell at first glance who is and who is not,' said a senior officer from the team.

'Not so,' said the Chief Doc.

'It must entail thorough examination and private questioning.'

'No, it's simple,' said the Doc. 'You catch him unawares and kiss him on the lips. If he shuts his eyes, he's queer. If he shuts your bastards, he's not.' (Much laughter.)

The Rear Admiral said, 'I must tell that one in the House.'

'Do you not think it unfit for the family to hear, Sir?' asked the 1st Lt.

'I mean the House of Commons.'

'Any hope I had of making flag rank just went down the tubes,' added the skipper.

HM S/M *Renown* had a problem with cockroaches on return from the USA. They were everywhere on the boat (except the Galley; they had taste). The engineers and medical staff got together to see just how resilient they were. SEVEN were collected and put in a large glass tube, the poison being used was included, the tube sealed and strapped to the Top Hat in the Reactor Compartment. The submarine went critical, and sailed on exercise.

Sixty-four days later we shut down, opened the Reactor Compartent, and removed the tube containing the cockroaches...only to discover FOURTEEN! This proves that they can live and breed in the Reactor Compartment, but not in the Galley. Wise creatures indeed.

Wardroom party, HM S/M *Renown*. Lots of high-ranking officers from the army, RAF, Marines and of course the navy. The Wardroom steward was Shuggy M, a tough little jock, from Port Glasgow, noted for the quantity of alcohol he could consume. The Jimmy was a pain in the Arris (what's new?) and led Shug a dog's life, but Shug cared not one jot.

The party was in full swing when the Jimmy turned in his chair, and, without rising, indicated his half-empty sherry glass to Shug.

'Sherry, M,' meaning for Shug to fill it up.

Shuggy, never slow to take advantage of a situation, said in his broad Scottish accent, 'Oh, cheers annat no,' and swallows the sherry.

The laughter could be heard in the forends.

Needless to say, he did not serve at any more Wardroom parties.

Salmonella: a real case of 'Delhi Belly'.

An S-class S/M had a wardroom steward who came back from holiday in India with salmonella, which, very quickly, spread throughout the boat. Several of the ship's company were left in Devonport and the boat sailed to Faslane. However, on the way up many more cases appeared. The long and the short of it was that, when the boat returned to Devonport, no leave would be granted until the whole ship's company produced three stool samples which were to be tested in the RNH Stonehouse laboratory.

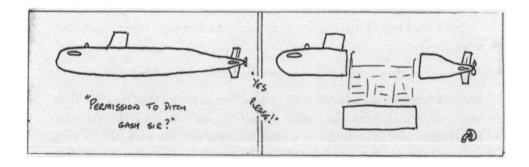
"PERMISSION TO DITCH GASH SIR?" Yes PLEASE!.

The laboratory was contacted by the submarine's medical staff, only to be informed that they did not work weekends and could only take fifty samples at a time. They were not happy when they discovered that they would work weekends until the samples from the submarine were analysed. The quantity would be, wait for it...375.

The trip from Faslane to Guz was a nightmare, with polythene bags full of stool samples stowed in every nook and cranny on the boat. However, on arrival at Devonport transport was arranged and the samples were taken to RNH Stonehouse laboratory.

The following week the results came through to the submarine. It did not make good reading. A new strain of salmonella had been detected in some, but not all, samples – good news. The bad news was that some of the samples were filled with foreign matter! Eight contained sausage; four, Mars bars; four, Branston Pickle; six came from the same person (how did they find that out?); two contained a mixture of Oxo cubes and gravy granules.

Anything for a Leave Pass eh?

Action had to be taken against the foreign-matter ratings, and stoppage of leave was ordered, to commence at the start of the next patrol.

Well, you have to laugh. Unless you work in Stonehouse laboratory.

A new stroppy Lt joined an S-class submarine alongside at Devonport. As he is passing the Wardroom Pantry he says to the stwd:

'Bring my breakfast to the bridge, and look smart about it.'

'Sir, the breakfast today is...' the stwd called after him.

'Just do as you are told,' came the very stern reply.

However, this was overheard by the captain, who said to the stwd, 'It's kippers today stwd, that right?'

'Yes, Sir, it's kippers.'

'Very good, take a kipper between two slices of bread to the bridge now, thank you.'

(5 minutes later.)

'Bridge, this is the captain, do you have your breakfast Lt?'

'Yes, Sir, I have it, but it's a kipper.'

'Well, eat it. I will be on the bridge directly to ensure you do, understand?'

He ate his breakfast in the Bunhouse after that.

For all you oldies out there, this will bring back some memories – some good, some bad. The Beckman analyser. As much use as a one-legged man in an ar*e-kicking contest. Au contraire, I hear you say. Well...

A Bomber at sea, with a problem:

'Fire in the Galley!'

The young chef had put twenty chickens in the oven, with the plastic bag of bits still in their rear orifices. The smell was enough to stun a gorilla. Draeger readings for Co, Co2, Arsene, Stibene, Hasbeen, Maureen and Irene were off the scale. The Beckman analyser readings were 1 per cent, 1 per cent, 1 per cent, 1 per cent, then it switched itself off!

'Must have got gassed,' was the verdict back aft.

The maintainer gave it the once over.

'In my professional view, it's tits up,' he announced.

The Doc made it P7Rc/i, Unfit for Chicken Inhalation.

Well, in the end the analyser went the way of the Dodo, and we got the Pye analyser. Hold me down.

One from the Sick Bay on a Bomber:

A missile mincer came to the Sick Bay with a slight skin complaint, saw the doctor, who prescribed a cream which name escapes me after so many years. The doctor, being new to the boat, left instructions for the MA to find the said cream, 2 per cent and dispense.

Not being able to find a 2 per cent tube of the cream he mixed two 1 per cent tubes and administered this solution to the patient.

As the patient made a full recovery nothing more was said. Doctor and patient were none the wiser.

This is a tale which has remained secret for the last twenty-five or so years, so names can now be named. HM S/M *Sceptre*, at sea on patrol: the usual pastimes were taken up; movies; cards; chess; Uckkers; inter-departmental quizzes; liar; dice; daily orders; bingo; and not forgetting dominoes.

The top table of S/Rs' mess favoured this game, and the rattle of the bones was heard many, many times. Throughout the patrol this rattle so annoyed one S/R, Tanzi Lees the wrecker, that in the early hours, when the mess was empty, he hid the dominoes. Fleet Chief Fred Voase was doing cartwheels, he was 'out of his bush'.

'If I find out who hid the bones, he will lose his rate and several fingers.'

The mess was scoured from stem to stern, port to starboard. No bones were found, and to make matters worse the song *Dem Bones, Dem Bones, Dem Dry Bones*, was very popular. Everywhere you went, the question was, 'Who hid the dominoes?'

Fred asked the chief doc, Toby Smyth, if he could administer the 'Truth Drug' to several suspects, or would teeth extraction be better? This was put to the mess members, without result. To give Tanzi his due, he never let on, and it was only long after the patrol that he owned up.

In one corner of the mess a wooden locker with four drawers was fitted, if you removed the top drawer there was a void inside, above it. Tanzi had masking-taped the dominoes into this void so unless you knew they were there, it was the last place you would look.

We all lost touch after leaving the boat, but I think Fred Voase is living in Berwick-upon-Tweed, so I hope he reads this. Now you know who hid the dominoes!

'Chef, there's a worm in this pie.'
'It's fat.'
'It ****** should be, it's eaten all the meat.'

Chapter Five

THE NEVER-ENDING STORY

EVEN MORE TIPS ON HOW TO BE A SUBMARINER:

- Turn off all the electrical power in the house and yell 'REACTOR SCRAM!' Sit in the dark for at least an hour. Time one of your guests to see how long it takes them to find the main power switch.

- If any light bulbs should inadvertently go out (i.e. see reactor scram above), make sure you hang danger tags on the light switches, fuses or breaker boxes, lamp plug sockets, home master breaker panels and also notify the local electricity company (manoeuvring) of what you are doing and demand their approval. Make sure both you and the wife sign the tags. Then tie a rope round yourself and have someone who would just as soon see you dead hold the rope in case you get electrocuted while changing the bulb.

- Make sure all your personal belongings will fit in a 2ftx2ft space that has lots of cables running through it.

Drills:

a.　Yell 'Torpedo!' and run through the house, knocking over everything that isn't bolted down.

b.　Yell 'Man overboard!' and throw the cat in the goldfish pond.

c.　Overflow the bath and yell 'Flooding in the bathroom!'

d.　Put your stereo headphones on (don't plug them in), stand in front of the stove and yell 'Action stations torpedo!'

e.　Install a very steep ladder in your living room so you can practise yelling 'Stand by, collision!' while the wife runs down the ladder as you time her.

Always shout 'Too slow, if it was real we'd all be dead!' if she doesn't manage to shut and clip the front door within four seconds of your first shout.

PERSONAL AD.....

Will the person who mistakenly shook the Chops 2 hours early for his watch halfway through the patrol, please collect their crate of beer from the Sound Room, it's starting to collect dust.

Control/Sound Room Reports.....

"Ops, Controller, Plasma panel's locked out, calling the maintainer."
"Controller, Ops, youv'e been watching Star Trek again, haven't you?"

****·<·*·*·*****·*****·*****·

Meanwhile, a little further along the passageway;

George Lavery to young RO,
                "Go on, ask me any question you like on part three, and I'll answer it."
                Aforementioned young RO spends a little time, deep in concentration, and then asks,
                "Why does my bird kick her ankles in the air when I'm bonkin' her? George, what are you doing on the deck, are you alright?"

S/R's mess, alongside at Faslane:

'Don't ask me!' exclaimed the wrecker.

So nobody did.

'Just don't expect me to explain,' he said, throwing himself rather too theatrically on to a mess seat.

Once again the gathered mess members didn't say a word.

'I just don't want to talk about it'.

The mess members seemed fairly happy with this.

'You just wouldn't believe it,' moaned the wrecker.

The mess showed no hurry to become believers. Nevertheless, with no prompting the wrecker expanded on the cause for his present, somewhat agitated, condition.

'Bloody regulators,' he gasped, as if asked to disown his beloved chisel-ended wheel spanner.

At this stage, I should explain that the wrecker and the regulators had a somewhat symbiotic relationship. They depended on one another; in so much as the wrecker needed the regulators or else he wouldn't have anything to talk about. Conversely, the regulators needed the wrecker to fill their charge sheets. I accept that some of my readers may not be of a naval background and will not be aware of who or what regulators are. That said, I feel it would be cruel to disturb this idyllic state of mind.

Somebody in the mess finally cracked, asking, 'What happened?'

'I'm not sure I want to talk about it.'

'Okay then,' said the somewhat relieved mess member, grateful for the potential reprieve.

'I don't know where they find them.' Obviously the wrecker had recovered from his reluctance to discuss his latest unfortunate encounter with the regulators. 'I tell you,' he continued, 'I just don't know where they find 'em.'

'Perhaps they follow you, wrecker?' offered a helpful mess member.

'Are you taking the ****?' countered the wrecker.

'Not at all, please continue.'

'Well...I had just been to the stores in the boat's Tilley, and on the way back I parked outside the Sick Bay, where the buses stop. I'd been there a couple of minutes, I was waiting for the LMA who needed some stuff, when there's a knock on the window. I look round and there's a reggy. I wound down the window...'

'You a bus then?' he says.

'You've not been doing this job long, have you? says I. 'Buses are a bit bigger and have got loads of windows in the sides. The Pusser's ones tend to be painted blue with RN on the side, bit of a give away if you ask me.'

'Bit of comedian, are we?' says the reggy.

'No, complete wrecker,' I replied. 'Now, at this, he takes out his notebook.'

'Right, let me see your ADP.'

'What?' says I.

'Your Pusser's driving licence,' says the fore mentioned regulator.

'ADP...PDL, how do they work that out? The navy would be better off investing in a troop of monkeys.'

'Right,' says he, 'What's your name?'

'Rutherford,' I said, 'and he writes it down! **** hell, I've had to remember it for forty-five years, he's only got to remember it till he gets back to the Reg Office, must be all of two minutes away.'

At this stage, those mess members still remaining awake had resigned themselves to a rather long afternoon, and they were not to be disappointed...

'Right, we'll see you in the Reg Office tomorrow, chief,' says he, pocketing his notebook.

'So this morning, entering the inner sanctum, I thought a bit of humour wouldn't go amiss.'

'Sorry you had to cancel the regulators' nativity play.'

'What?' said a bemused leading regulator.

'Yeah, I heard you had trouble finding three wise men.'

The wrecker chuckled at his little jibe; several mess members stopped filling in their last will and testament forms and politely laughed.

'I also mentioned they would have trouble finding a virgin.'

'Oh, very good Wrecker,' said one member, on his way to the mess door.

'No bloody sense of humour them reggies,' observed the wrecker.

At this stage the remaining mess member took a sharp knife to his wrists.

The comeuppance of this particular run-in with the navy's chosen few was that he was confined on board for two weeks, which, while a pleasant respite for the much maligned regulating staff, did little for the morale of the on board senior rates who were effectively a trapped audience for the wrecker's renewed rantings.

'Did I tell you' enquired the wrecker, 'about the leading regulator who got a WRN into trouble? Yeh, he told her she could park in the captain's billet on three berth'.

While he convulsed over his little jibe, the entrapped mess members were left thinking that the S/Rs' leadership course wasn't such a bad option.

'I've got another one,' quipped the wrecker.

'Oh goody,' sighed the mess members.

'Did you hear about the reggy who trapped a WREN. After a night in the Trident Club, he's walking her back to the WREN's quarters when she says, "treat me rough". So, he picked her up for a haircut and gave her seven days nines. God, I kill myself sometimes,' laughed the wrecker.

HMS *Conqueror.*

HMS *Conqueror.*

'You don't do a lot for us either,' said a dismayed mess member.

'No, wait, I've got another.'

A load groan.

'What's the difference between the Master at Arms and the M1?'

Deadly silence.

'You can turn off the M1!' said the wrecker, collapsing into fits of laughter.

Once the wrecker was allowed ashore again, things quickly reverted back to normal. On day two of his release he was caught smoking in a non-smoking area.

'Can't you read?' enquired a leading regulator, pointing at a no smoking sign.

'Course I can, that's why I'm a chief tiff and not a leading regulator.'

'What a w**ker,' said the wrecker, as he regaled mess members with this latest episode of woe at the hands of the navy's finest.

'The doctor had to bring down one of his testicles from Inverness. Anyway, where was I, ah yes, I finished up in front of the Master at Arms. "How did you know my right eye was a glass eye?" he asked. "There's a spark of humanity in it" says I. Oh my god, you should have seen his face.'

Well, the wrecker did see the face of the Master at Arms, quickly followed by the base's 1st Lt, then, to round things off, the submarine's commanding officer.

HMS *Conqueror*.

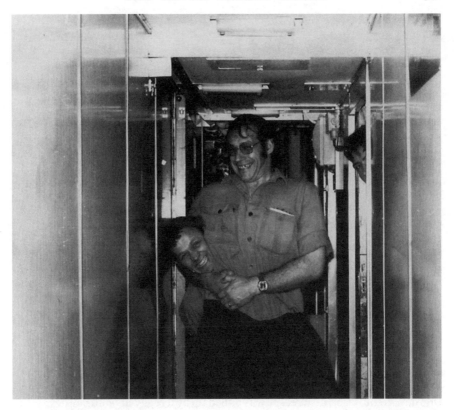

'Helping hand.'

Needless to say, the wrecker found himself living on board again. The wrecker didn't accept this imposition with his usual goodwill.

'Did I tell you?' the wrecker asked the mess, 'I heard the doctor talking to a couple of his mates the other day. They were talking about who they would prefer to operate on. One reckoned electricians were best, because when you open them up it's just boards. You pull out the broken one and pop in a new one. "No, no" says the second one, "its got to be engineers, all their pipes are colour coded." "I disagree," said our Doc, "regulators are by far the easiest to operate on, only two parts, mouth and an a**e-hole, and they're interchangeable."'

The wrecker slipped under the table in hysterics. The listening mess members wondered what the chances of getting a swap draft with somebody on an S-boat would be.

The story had a strange, elegiac, but some might say fitting end.

Outside the galley, HMS *Renown*.

One day, in the base, the wrecker was pulled up by a reggy in plain clothes.

'Stay in long enough and they'll probably give you a uniform like me,' he quipped.

Now, for reasons still to be determined, the wrecker was with his rather attractive daughter, who had a job in the base. She felt she had to apologise to the reggy for her father's inappropriate remarks. Well, one thing led to another and before you could say four valve chest, they were an item. The wrecker was beside himself, especially when eight months later his nubile eighteen-year-old daughter announced she intended to marry her leading regulator; poetic justice indeed.

The mess ran a book on the contents of his father-of-the-bride speech, although nobody collected. The day passed without incident, the wrecker beamed and was without a doubt the world's proudest father. He spoke fondly of his new son-in-law and was even pictured sharing a drink with the Master at Arms, one that it was rumoured he had bought.

Funny old world...

Chapter Six

EDUCATIONAL SUPPLEMENT

STILL MORE TIPS:

- Loudly repeat back everything anyone says to you.

- Watch only unknown movies with no major stars and show it at the same time for a week. For extra realism, have your guests vote on which movie to watch. Then watch a different one.

- Put a complicated padlock on your shed door and wear the key on a lanyard around your neck.

- Monitor all home appliances hourly, recording on log sheets all vital information (i.e. plugged in, lights come on when doors open, and so on).

- Have one of the guests draw a labelled diagram of the house plumbing system. Make several unreadable xeroxed copies of this. Then get the guests to identify and find valves on the system using the copies.

- Serve cold food on cold days and hot food on hot days. Serve breakfast at the end of a hard day's work, and a good roast dinner just as everyone wakes up. Then alternate the routine.

- Graph all tea-bag and toilet-roll usage. For more authenticity, pin up copies of the graphs on to every available space.

- Ensure that the water boiler is connected to a device that provides water at a flow rate that varies quickly from a torrent to a weak trickle, with the temperature alternating rapidly from two to ninety-five degrees.

● Use only spoons that hold a minimum of half a cup at a time.

● Make sure every water valve in your home has two backups, in line, which must all be operated to obtain water.

SOME COLLECTIVE NOUNS:
A thicket of TSs
A clutch of stokers
A rack of WEOs
A wedge of chefs
A coagulation of doctors
A band of ROs
A mince of nav queens
A platter of stewards
A tube of forendies
A stock of SAs
A folio of navigators
An album of polaroids
A battery of greenies
A pen of officers
A cloud of RPOs
An earful of UCs
An erh of DMEOs
A unit of 1st Lts

SOME MORE COLLECTIVE NOUNS:
A bevy of OAs
A troop of Cox'ns
A flood of fwd stokers
A dhoby of fwd stokers
A grump of TASOs
A fiddle of MEOs
A divan of PWEOs
A clump of UCs
A heard of UC1S
A circus of captains
A bracket of foreplanesmen
A rectum of SOs
A shower of primary samplers
A binful of gashmen

Anyone knowing the plural of sausage contact the supply officer!

DOC: 'I suggest you run two miles every morning and two miles each evening.'
AB R: 'Will that make me feel better?'
DOC: 'No, but by the end of the week you'll be twenty-eight miles away.'

On asking the grumpy corner ratings what they thought about blowing slop drain and sewage, their representative, LWEM C, said that they didn't mind in the slightest as it was due to their continuous and regular on-watch showers.

Which ex-*Warspite* greenie-type officer thought he'd got away with tasting the white wine in the wardroom? He wasn't on the wine list by the way.

The LSA on the aft planes was heard to say, when coming back through the clouds: 'Ship control switch off the no-smoking lights, unfasten seat belts, serve the in-flight meal and I'll be around with the duty frees soon.'

LSA G is in the RNR, he's a jumbo pilot in real life.

REVIEW BOOK CLUB

PLANESMEN REVENGE

At last the book of many quips
enabling the much malined
planesmen to fight back.
Classics such as:
Who put this trim on..RUBIC..?

"How's the Trim?".."we'll let
you know as soon as we get to
within 50' of our depth bracket!

"I wonder if the skipper will let
us ventilate while we are up here?"

THE HMS RESOLUTION RADIOACTIVE LIQUID WASTE DISPOSAL LOG. 1990

Compiled:- .... HALL

The difinitive work, a masterpiece a must for any fiction Section.

TRIM WITH NUN

A must for every ship control,
Takes you from the easy!
Trimming in a straight line.
To the difficult?
Turning a corner while pumping
shit and Brine, bollocking the
planesmen and! firing an XBT

ALSO AVAILABLE ON CASSETTE

ROY ON SIGNS

The definative work for any-one
with a message to put across
Who could forget

....BE THERE OF FUCK YER

...BY SATURDAY 0930 OR ELSE
IT'S IN THE FUCKIN BIN

There is a special chapter
on signs for children...

WORK OUT WITH POUNDER

MC LOWER LEVEL CALISTHENICS AND AEROBICS.

WITH

THE BLUE EMPEROR

SHOWS YOU:

'HOW TO STAY YOUNG AND BEAUTIFUL'

' HOW TO LIE ABOUT IT, IF YOU CANT STAY YOUNG AND BEAUTIFUL.

Comes Complete with wooley leg warmers and scrotal support.

THE CHURCHILL MENAGERIE

The Parriste (Wittus Atius)

This is a very unusual creature, usually frequenting that frightening jungle 'manco-vering'. By nature a shy creature, it very rarely goes out to forage with the rest of his species. He prefers to spend his time at home with his family.

Place to spot: scran queue or on the jetty when the boat sails.

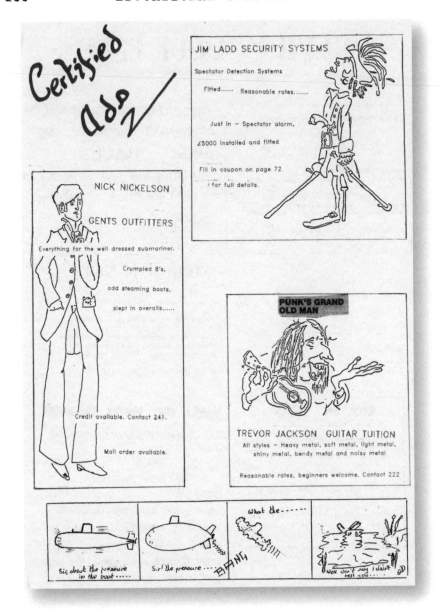

The Eshelnail (Tiredus Headus)

Probably the most rarely seen creature in the menagerie. Only leaving the nest twice a day, at feeding times. Without food, this animal would probably spend four to five weeks hibernating. Easily recognised by the pillow on his head and mattress on his back.

Place to spot: J/R's bunk space.

The Hayward Lion (Misterbigus) (Goingus Thankcgodus)
Reputedly the king of the beasts, but really a wolf in sheep's clothing (I think). Spends all of his waking hours prowling the menagerie, striking terror into the Dumbus Sailorus and enforcing Hayward's Law of 'I'm always right'. Don't be misled by the glinting eyes and endearing smile, this beast can be dangerous when aroused, especially at harbour stations.

Place to spot: behind doors/round corners.

The Chatterbox (Boringus Bastardus)
Found anywhere a dit needs spinning. One of the Broadbelt family of boring monkeys. The chatterbox could talk the hind legs off a rocking horse. Resembles a mandrake in so much that he is very colourful, but that is his only good point. Do not try to black cat this man, he's done it before.

Place to spot: everywhere.

The Kelly Bird (Gimmitus Moneyus)
One of the vulture family that hangs around and prays off unsuspecting ratings. Will do anything for money. If seen, take immediate action drill. DO NOT TRUST THIS BIRD.

Place to spot: two deck, lower, forward.

The Mansergh Rabbit (Hoperforus Humpus)
A true member of the rabbit family with one exception, this is the only rabbit that never ever gets a bit.

Place to spot: WI Meeting.

All at Sea on HMS Repulse *(continued)*:
The boat is at sea and the starboard side of the Control Room are doing something paradoxically called Attack Teams. The port side of the compartment look on, nonplussed. I mean, we never seem to discover if they actually hit anything. Anyway, XO is doing famously. Orders are delivered with a firmness and clarity which almost defy description. The enemy, plainly, is fairly lined up for the kill.

XO: '...and range, ten thousand miles.'
CAPTAIN (hacked-off): 'YARDS!' (Thinks, 'for Gawd's sake.')

During the AMS1 exercise fire, LT B burst, Phoenix-like, through the exercise flame and exercise smoke, complaining of the lack of communications with the Control Room. It was noted that he was not wearing an EBS and that his shirt sleeves were rolled up.

Note for Part Threes:

You take all exercises seriously and play them as for real. When ordered to do so (or when you start to cough up pieces of your respiratory system) you wear EBS. Moreover, you roll down your shirt sleeves to prevent safeguard burns should the real thing ever happen. (Down the snake and back to square one, Sir.)

The starboard crew rider in CPO M R, was seen in the S/Rs' heads trying to dispense liquid soap from an Automatic Emergency Light.

The MCC White Rat, the source of the above dit, reports, additionally, the following:

'Button-crusher' Y E is standing on three deck outside the open MCC door after a recent fire exercise, wailing:

'And does this CO2 extinguisher belong to you, NAV Pooftas?'

Note to Part Threes: The Nav Centre is on one deck in the vicinity of the Control Room.
       Another note to Part Threes: Y E is your actual Part Three co-ordinator.

The Cox'n was explaining the use of the top-up tube on the escape suits during one of his ever popular submarine escape 'everything-you-need-to-know' lectures:

AB C: 'Top up, bloody top up, I want stays up!'

A little later, during the same lecture, when the Cox'n was explaining the use of the cleverly concealed little plastic whistle:

AB C: 'A whistle, a bloody whistle. Bobbing about in the middle of the Atlantic, America, a thousand miles that way, UK 600 miles over there, and I've got a bloody whistle!'

On a more reassuring note, the new escape suits have got a 'boat' stowed away in the port leg of the suit. During my last escape training session I ripped the starboard leg to bits to see if there was a helicopter in there so I could fly home.

AN ODE

REPENT, REPENT, It's Imminent,
The Skipper he doth say,
We've been at sea for forty odd,
So whats a couple of days,
But why the cry from 3 deck comes,
When will they leave us be,
When will that heap Revenge be fixed,
To join us here at sea,
Until the committee they have met,
To talk of trouser legs,
But until then boys you'll have to do,
With mushies and grapefruit segs.

There's people there, there's people here,
But whats that boys, were out of beer,

Lighter fuel is now extinct,
And all we eat is out of tins,
Gash bags are in short supply,
And everyone wonders why,
So here we sit from day to day,
Waiting for someone to say,
Come home boys your time is done,
We hope you've had a lot of fun,
FREDDIE FREON is everywhere,
They ask us not to smoke,
One little pleasure we enjoy,
we hope this a joke.

There's people there, there's people here,
Buts what's that boys, were out of beer,

Let us have some rounds, the HODS they shout,
To boost the boys moral,
Turn too each day during the dogs,
We shout HIP HIP HOORAY,
But wait we cry, we've got no gear,
No flash or scotchbrite that is clear,
Dont worry chaps the HODS they say,
We are sure you'll find a way,
So here we are all at sea,
One in three and thats the way we love to be.

anonymouse.

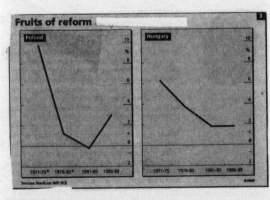

Graph II

Showing Dramatic fall
in Teabag usage in Warsaw
Pact... after introduction
of Gossa

a dazzling display

Smudge spelt out a four-letter word – correctly!

Seen in the Resolution-class Sea Qualification Book, Part C – Submarine Safety and General Submarine Questions (Q 32):

What action would you take on discovering fire in an O2 generator?
    Answer by OS S: 'Suffocate it with an electric blanket.'

The boat heads for Rhu Narrows. SO(D) is on the casing with the SO:

'For exercise man overboard!'
    A pyrotechnic is ejected from the aft SSE.
    'Oh s**t, now we're on fire,' wailed the SO(D).

The lads were discussing sex – what else – in the dinning hall.
    AB F: 'I thought multiple organisms were them funny grenade launchers at the front of them Russian destroyers.'

Review Book Club

THIS MONTH'S SPECIAL OFFERS

WORK 2 OUT WITH LAKELAND

Control Room Calisthenics and Aerobics
With
The Blue Emperor

Shows You;

How to stay young and beautiful
How to extract yourself from the Alarm Panel

Comes Complete with Woolly Leg Warmers and Scrotal
Support

£15:50

THE NOBLE ART OF SELF DEFENCE
BY
PAT GAGALLAGAHER

Features;

Bottling
Eye Poking
Goolie Biting
Basic Knuckle Duster Maintenance

All aspects of the course taught to advanced

Millwall Fan Club Standards.

From the award-winning Series,
"COOKING WITH NOBBY"
comes our latest,
"COOKING WITH SENNA PODS"
Yes folks 1000 things to do with Senna Pods
in the kitchen, and then afterwards in the

Bathroom

TEACH YOURSELF
TRIMMING

All you ever wanted to
know about trimming, now
in one pocket?sized
book.
Readers start with
mastering the basic dive
trim, then progress on to
the difficulties of shit
pumping, pumping Brine,
turning corners, answer-
the phone etc.
An absolute
must for any SCOOW.

£9:15p

Available to the General Public at Last

WATSON ON PHOTOGRAPHY

All aspects of Amatuer Photography
covered in this breath taking Book

Nudes, Standing Nudes, Sitting
Nudes, Nudes Outdoors, Nudes Indoors,
Nudes on Bikes, Nudes Hanging From
Trees. Book available to you, in
Plain Brown Wrapper, complete with
spectacles and Raincoat.

£16:25

ORDER FORM

Please Rush Me....... copies of .... @.........per copy. Ienclose cheque/ postal
order for £.........
I understand that if I have not received any books within
six months, then I have been seen off.

signed ....

Chapter Seven

SUBMARINERS IN THE REAL NEWS

STILL MORE TIPS:

- Spend as much time as possible indoors and avoid sunlight. Only view the world through the spy hole on your front door. For added realism, don't let family members or friends use the spy hole unless they are 'periscope' qualified.

- Buy a garbage compactor and use it once a week. Store your rubbish in the other side of your bathtub.

- Put lubricating oil in your air humidifier instead of water and set it to high.

- Don't do your washing at home. Pick the most crowded laundromat you can find.

- Leave the lawnmower running in your living room for six hours a day to simulate the proper noise level. To make things more realistic, take readings every four hours. Report these to your wife.

- Once a month, take every major appliance completely apart and then put them back together. Ensure you have parts left over. If desired, when finished report to your wife 'vacuum cleaner up and running'. Even if it isn't.

- Use eighteen scoops of coffee per pot and allow it to sit for five or six hours before drinking. Never wash any coffee cups. To ensure accuracy, never have enough cups.

Store your eggs in your garage for two months and then scramble a dozen each morning.

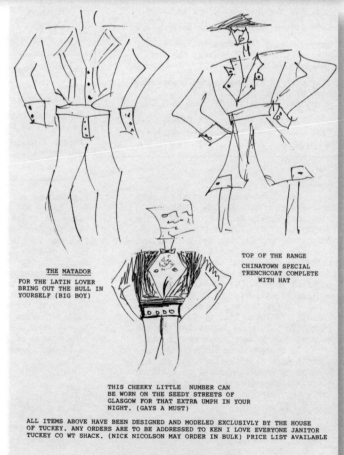

GOSSIP

We would hate to say anything nasty about people...as you may have noticed...but in the case of Bogey we feel obliged to make an exception. As you may recall, the dart game was what might be described as a racket. We only point this out in the interests of fair play. The fact that we got nowhere with 'em has bog all to do with it.................While on the subject of the garden fete, I like the style of the Supply Officer. Play the game, and if you win you get your money back....

Jimmy Green, better known as plank seems to get plenty of hours in his cart. We don't know what he does there but from now on his bag can be called plank too, it's that stiff......

Frank Quinlan, apart from thinking of buying up a beer cannery, has an answer for critics of his focussing. "It's not so much out of focus, as in focus too much for the uneducated eye to grasp..."

Taff Davies joins the over forties....

Anyone having the words to 'Stewball', please contact Taff Davies, the Tom Jones of white watch.....

"Why are you hitting yourself over the head with that hammer, Ben?"
"Duh, cos it isn't half nice when I stop"

Overheard from the Systems Console...
"You can't crack me, I'm too stupid..."

* * * * * | * * * * *

"THINKS" THE SETS JUST COMING ALONG FINE NOW MY BOY, THINK I'LL TRIM IT TOMORROW"   'BOY ITS A HARD LIFE' SIGH!

LOST AND FOUND

Anyone knowing the whereabouts of 250 cups is asked to contact LRO Knott.

Anyone knowing the whereabouts of LRO Knott is asked to contact 250 cups.

Anyone finding the Beckman analyser can keep it..........

* * * * * * * * * *

A FABLE

Once upon a time ther was a very kind and holy man. He was completely kind, and wholly holy. He lived in the jungle in Africa, where his favourite occupation was tarring and feathering himself, an art he had learned from his father in India, who used to tar and feather himself to gain attention at cocktail parties, as he was a lousy conversationalist.

Anyway, one day he thought to himself, "I think I'll go for a walk in the forest, good job it isn't black because that record gives me the pip."

As he came into a clearing, he spied a lion directly in front of him moaning in agony. Embedded in the lion's paw was a huge thorn. In spite of his fear, the holy man was touched with compassion, and taking his courage in both hands and pausing only long enough to shake the bits from his left trouser leg, he removed the thorn from the lion's paw. The lion licked his face with friendliness, and bounded away uttering little cries of joy.

A few weeks later the holy man was again walking in the forest, when a lion bounded in front of him. He was rigid with terror, until the lion padded forward and licked his face. AS he was thanking his lucky stars, the lion opened it's mouth and tore him to bits. It was a different lion......

Ecch

Dear Doctor,

       I am a wimp, but I want so much to be
Rambo-like and macho like all of the other guys.

       I work out and exercise every day along
with the other would-be Arnold Swzxaniggers (the
guy with all the muscles) but at the end of the
day I'm too knackered to put the bike away.

       What do you advise ?

Junior Rates Dining Hall;

Fond memories of last Index;

MEM 1, " Who's that, doing all the gobbing off
     " on the uderwater telephone?"

MEM 2, " X.O. ; he's talking to another boat."

MEM 1, " Oh well, save wear and tear on the mike,
    I suppose."

TS 1" Does the TAS ever buy any fags?"

TS 2" I dunno, but see that silver chain that
    leads into his pocket, I'll bet there's
    a padlocked packet on the end of it! "

Is it true that Nobby the clacker basher, is on a
back-hander from the canteen?

Is it true that the Captain wants to swap jobs with
Robby E , 'cos he's got a better number than him?

Is it tue that Brian Mathers thinks Merryl Streep is
"not bad looking for a woman?"

Is it true that Pete (grumps) Timms is after the XO's

Great Unanswered Questions Of Our Time.

1. Why is it that when Naval Officers get bored
   they give the troops jobs to do ?

Is it true that Pete (grumps) Timms is after the XO's
job as well?

Is it true that the Chops auditioned for the part of
Mickey the Monkey in Supercar?

Is it true that Joe(old man time) Bromwich, is the
oldest Teddy Boy in 10 Navies?

If Harry Fazal worked in a flour mill, would he kick
  up dirt money?

Brian's got a dress for the Sod's Opera. One of his
Wife's? No, it just happened to fit him. mmm.

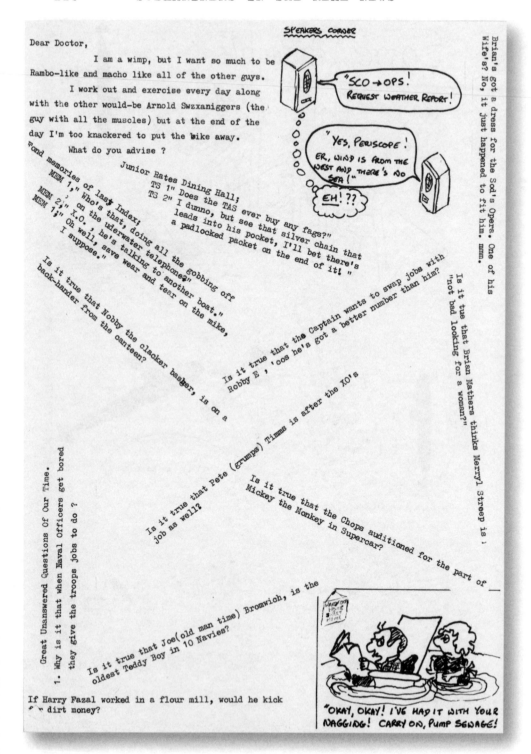

SPEAKERS CORNER

"SCO → OPS !
REQUEST WEATHER REPORT !"

"YES, PERISCOPE !
ER, WIND IS FROM THE
WEST AND THERE'S NO
SEA !"

EH ! ??

"OKAY, OKAY ! I'VE HAD IT WITH YOUR
NAGGING ! CARRY ON, PUMP SEWAGE !"

SPEAKERS CORNER

"I HAVE A TADPOLE CONTACT SIR, AT RED 40"

"YAWN!"

"TELL ME WHEN IT TURNS INTO A FROG!"

SODA

THIS CONSTITUTES AN OFFICAL CHALLENGE UNDER RULE 4 B

MEMBERS NOT ABLE TO PRODUCE THEIR BADGE WITH-IN 9 SECONDS OF READING THIS ARE TO BUY THE NEAREST MAGAZINE STAFF A PINT-----!

CHEERS .... MIND HOW YOU GO

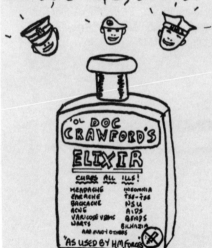
REVIEW QUIZ

ENTER NOW?-- STAR PRIZES---- ENTER NOW

All you have to do is answer the following questions;

Question 1.

    Who said, on hearing that the VIP was John Stanley, (Who?')

"Oh goody, so much better than a boring old Admiral like FOSM......pump 50 galls to the after trim."

Question 2.
    Guess the OOW;
SCOOW" Shall I pipe heads and bathrooms back in use?"
OOW" No, let 'em suffer."

Question 3.
    Guess the officer;
"The X.O. is just the Captain's tool."

Question 4.
    Guess the two officers;
1   "These are delicious."
2   "Mmm, crunch, mmm, munch, etc,"

Bonus points for guessing what they are talking about.

Place your answers in the Captain's empty chocolate mint biscuit bottle by Friday.

    Editor's decision is
            FINAL

BUNK FOR RENT IN MUCH SOUGHT AFTER 3 DECK PICTURESQUE 3 DECK VILLAGE. H.C. LH PB SOB PT CONTACT R.S. 205

How's the atmosphere Doc?

Fine Dir,.. Just fine....

oh shit ....

THE CONTROL ROOM JUST AFTER THE BEWITCHING HOUR. THE CHIEF DOC SETTLES
HIMSELF INTO THE AFTERPLANES SEAT. AFTER SETTING HIS ALARM CLOCK FOR

0345

CAPTAIN : Goodnight doc!
CH Doc : Goodnight sir, are going to sleep???
Captain : NO but you fuckin are!

Depressed, suicidial

Planesman Anonymous
Phone 222.
WERE ONE OF OUR HIGHLY TRAINED
CONSULTANTS WILL GIVE YOU A
BOLLOCKING ABOUT KEEPING ON DEPT
REMEMBER THERE'S NO SUCH THING AS
AN EXPLANESMAN.

      The CH Doc reckons that if you put dogs on the afterplanes. The
owners would be had up for cruelty.(who said the RS was dogs)

A POLISHED PERFORMER

YOU'LL BE ALL OVER THE PLACE WITHOUT US

0405: S/R ANNEX:
CH Doc staggers in, visibly broken after the middle on the after planes.
"It's a pity all the watches can't be like that!"
S/R's : "What Good !"
CH Doc : "No, Fuckin over !"

THE VIEW FROM HERE

LT CDR FINNY SEVERLY CHASTISES A CREW MEMBER HE FOUND DEFACING A GRAPH.

COX'N NUNN GUARDS THE ENTRANCE TO THE SECRET HIDEAWAY OF THE MAN KNOWING THE WHEREABOUTS OF THE LAST TEABAG.

CREW MEMBERS SEARCH FOR THE LAST TEABAG

ANXIOUS NAVAL WIVES AWAIT NEWS OF RESOLUTIONS RETURN

For the Moment, the Shock Is Limited

The Legendary

Cabbage Patch Submariner

Special features:-

* one eye for watching vidio's,
* one small ear so vidio's, films
  and music as to be played really
  LOUD!
* special feature hands and
  arms for slamming doors.

Just press his tummy and listen to him
drip about the food, sea time, the other crew etc.......

comes complete with optional 'T' shirt.

THINGS YOU'VE SAID OR DONE...............

Overheard in the JR's mess,

Archy "I may not be able to spell
in Scrabble but I do know how to play."

* * * * * *

Paddy 'N' down in the showers, as usual
Reggie's packing cardboard.

Reggie "shit, got me watch wet."
Paddy   "that's OK mine says 'waterproof
to 300ft'and I had a shower at 600ft the
other night."
Reggie ....Stunned?

* * * * * *

Overheard in the Control Room,
1st Lt to Doctor:- "you don't want to
keep pulling it Doc., it might come off."

* * * * * *

Bonny to Daisey Mays.....
"Can you unblock my sink?" Daisey looks,
then pulls the plug out. ? ? ?

* * * * * *

Soapy 'C' "as I was saying, I think the
Nimrods are being fitted with 'Sting Ray'
its a super version of the Mk46 torpedo."
Paddy 'P' "Yeh, its wire guided, isn't it?"

* * * * * *

In the JR's mess:-
Pete Elwood "we're having a 'be nice to
Steven' day, today (Black Mac)."
Glen Spriglet "we never have a 'be nice
to Spriglet' day."
Pet replies "your never up long enough."

* * * * * *

At a union meeting at top of TG RM
during (laugh) turn to.
Beano "I hear the Navvy has called his
sprog 'Megan Jane' ."
Splash "what, Megga Jane?"
Slinky "Is that the same as 'Big Nancy'?"

* * * * * *

Simon "When are you going to get the
Chief Tiff certified ?"
Glen "He is, already, I think."

* * * * * *

DMEO was heard to say....
"I'm thinking of building up for
another season, now." (refering, I
think, to rugby) "though I am
beginning to feel a bit OLD."

* * * * * *

MEO(D) "COW's turn to wet the tea."
COEA   "No chance sir, I'm not making
any 'till the trip home."
MEO(D) "What would happen if we all
said that?"
Spud M "We'd get a fucking lot of tea
on the way home."

* * * * * *

MEO(D) (after wetting the tea for the
watch) was extolling the virtues of
powdered milk:-
"5 PINTS, is about the best, by the time
you've mixed it up, you can't taste the
difference. In fact I've even had
K 5 PINTS on my cornflakes."
Spud, from the other end of manoeuvring,
"Christ, how many cornflakes does he have?"

* * * * * *

FULL MAIN BROADCAST .. (for those who
missed the original)
"D'ya heah there, Navigator speaking,
I'm beginning to sound like a tape
recording (who is arguing) again there
is no news and nothing more to say,
that is all."
(we think he should have used a blank tape")

* * * * * *

Who are they discussing?
Chief Doc "...yes, I know, sir, I've
got children of my own."
MEO "What like that?"
Chief Doc, a noncommittal "well"
MEO "With a little beard and a bald patch."

* * * * * *

Talking about 'white rabbits' and the
1st of the month Tony Skiggs said,
"the only white rabbits IXX I've seen
this trip is officers hopping about in
their white overalls,"
Who was on watch but El FRITH.

* * * * * *

On Friday 24 February 1956 HMS *Acheron* was the focus of a 'Sub Sunk' operation. She was operating off the coast of Greenland and failed to send a surfacing signal. The BBC broadcast that the submarine was missing and very anxious naval families gathered at the submarine's depot ship at Rothesay.

This dreadful incident was made worse, if that were possible, by the fact that HMS *Affray*, a submarine of the same class, had been lost with all hands just five years previously in the English Channel.

Luckily, in this case the surfacing signal was eventually received five hours later. The POTS blamed sun-spot activity.

A young Bob Cantly was an Able Seaman on board the *Acheron*, and when he returned to Aberdeen on leave, just after this incident, his mum Alice took him to the local cinema. As was the tradition in those days, he was in rig. Before the film started the Pathé News was shown, and lo and behold HMS *Acheron* was shown coming alongside the depot ship at Rothesay, and up through the foward hatch came young Bob, resplendent in submarine sweater, steaming bats and hair of an unfashionable length.

Mrs Cantly stood up and, in front of a crowded cinema, said in a very loud voice, 'Robert, look at the state of that jumper and your hair...bringing shame on the family, how could you? And on the news as well...oh the shame...what will the neighbours say?'

Mothers – bless 'em.

Daily Record

SAT FEB 25 1956

SCOTLAND'S NATIONAL NEWSPAPER

2ᴰ No. 18,820.

All Rothesay hushed

WIVES OF SUB. MEN WAIT FIVE HOURS IN TERROR

Shani is in!

Mrs. Seymore . . . "His first and last submarine."

FOR five hours yesterday, heart-broken women in Rothesay waited and prayed.

The submarine Acheron was feared missing off Greenland with 60 men aboard — many of them from Rothesay itself.

Wives wept in misery after Navy messengers brought bad news ashore from the Acheron's depot ship in Rothesay Bay.

Town hushed

The Acheron had been due to send a signal from off Greenland at 10.5 in the morning.

But no signal came, and the last message had been: "Preparing to dive."

The Navy's "Sub Sunk" message was flashed. The B.B.C.

broadcast. The womenfolk were told.

Weeping women crowded the Rothesay quayside, looking out to the depot ship Adamant for news. Shops closed.

The whole town was hushed.

Then, in the afternoon, faint signals from Acheron were picked up.

The Acheron s u r f a c e d. And, after all the five hours' tension, sent this matter-of-fact signal: "Will carry on patrol. Will be seeing you."

Why did it all happen? Cosmic rays from the sun "killed" Acheron's first signals.

Last night a thanksgiving church service was held in Rothesay.

And, down at Hayling Island, on the South Coast of England, fair - haired, 30-year-old Mrs. Isobel Hay broke down and wept.

Her husband, 32-year-old Lieut.-Commander Peter Hay, is commander of the Acheron.

As little Shellie (four) and Catriona (one) played on the

hearthrug Mrs. Hay had to pretend—to herself, almost—that nothing was wrong.

In blue slacks and sweater she went about her housework . . . But picturing her young husband trapped in a submarine at the bottom of an Arctic sea.

Several times she end her father phoned a nearby submarine base.

At 4 p.m. the phone went again and Mrs. Hay feared to answer it.

But this time the message was: "Acheron is in radio contact."

They cheer

Aboard the depot ship Adamant in Rothesay Bay a great cheer went up — and the good news swept through the town.

In her cottage at Sheriff's Croft, Rothesay, Mrs. Colina Marshall (29), wept with relief and joy.

She had been feeding her month-old baby girl when a Navy man knocked at her door after lunch, to say that Acheron was missing. She fainted at the news.

Her husband is Chief Petty Officer Jimmy Marshall of the Acheron.

"I've never been through anything like that in my whole life," she said afterwards. "I've never prayed so hard and so long in my life."

With her was her minister, praying for Acheron's crew.

Mrs. Sheila Seymore (21), wept bitterly when she got the first news.

She and her husband Peter (also 21), are married only seven months—they met when she was in the WRNS and she came to Rothesay a fortnight ago.

Her eyes still red from weeping, Mrs. Seymore said: "This is Peter's first submarine—and his last, if I've anything to do with it. I'll ask him to leave the Submarine Service."

Other newspaper headlines relating to the incident included:

'LOST' SUB SENDS A SIGNAL

THE 'LOST' SUB ACHERON BACK IN ROTHESAY

16-HOUR 'WATCH' ON SUB'S RADIO

Chapter Eight

THE STRANGE CASE OF THE MISSING BURMA CROSS AND THE SHRUNKEN HEAD

EVEN FURTHER TIPS:

- Install four more toilets in your bathroom. Serve greasy meals, and demand the entire family go to the bathroom together.

- Buy bunk beds (three beds high), and convert the narrowest hallway in your home into a bedroom.

- Just for fun, rig 150-PSI air to the bottom of all toilets. Hold a lottery to determine who gets to control the air valves.

- Knock a glass of water out of someone's hand and yell 'WATER SPILLAGE!' Shout at them the entire time they clean it up, tell them how worthless they are, and then do it again.

- Give your wife more free time. All the ironing goes under the mattress.

- Ask for 'permission to enter', whenever you go into the kitchen.

- Replace all doorways with windows so that you have to step up AND duck to go through them.

- Rope off a small area of your living room, turn up the heating, put on a suit made of garbage bags and mill around inside the roped-off area for an hour with a plastic bag tied securely around your head.

- Paint the windows of your car black. Make your wife stand up through the sunroof and give you directions on where to drive. Drive through as many big puddles as possible.

- Start every story with, 'This is no-shit...'

A letter written by an Able Seaman resulted in the correspondence across the next few pages. This involves the true story of a General Service Medal, tucked away in the safety of a shrunken head, that went missing in the most humourous yet unfortunate of ways. The chaos that followed shows the navy at its bureaucratic best.

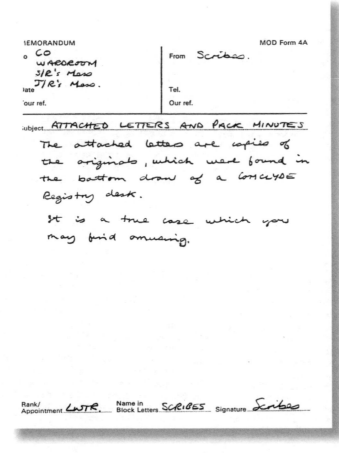

HMS DREADNOUGHT
at Sea

The Commanding Officer
HMS DREADNOUGHT   22 October   1973

S.R.

1.   I regret to report the events leading up to and the subsequent loss of my
General Service Medal (Malay Peninsula).

2.   I was given the medal whilst serving in HMS REPULSE in 1967, and a home
was found for it inside a shrunken head converted into a cigarette box which
I obtained by swopping two tots and a Submarine cap tally with a drunken
Marine sergeant in a Borneo Long House, we both being guests of the Seventh
Gurkha Rifles.   After my return to UK the shrunken head with the medal inside
was transfered to an unlocked glass case in my house in Helensburgh.   Here
it reposed in peace for 12 months and would no doubt continue to do so had
there not been a christening party celebrating the birth of our third child.
At some time during the party one of our more witty underwater guests removed
the shrunken head from the glass case (complete with medal), wrapped it in a
napkin, and set about it with a bottle of milk.   On being asked by my wife what
he thought he was doing he replied "I'm feedin' the effing baby".   (In all
fairness to him the baby, then only three days old, was a bit wizened, but my
wife, who was sober and not feeling very well at the time was not amused.
On returning from work next day it had come to pass that a decision at
wife/eldest daughter/gang of nosey vindictive women level had been taken to
get rid of my shrunken head by way of the Helensburgh Rural District Council
Mobile Garbage Disposal Vehicle.   However this was not to be.   I removed the
medal from it's place of rest and laid it on the shelf, still inside the cupboard.
To cover my losses I exchanged the head with a neigbour a CERA (P) for two tots,
two pints and a Rover 75 workshop manual (1953) and considered I had made a profit.
Had the Tiffy arranged a transplant, he would have profited too.

3.   My eldest daughter, then nine years old, and a fully fledged member of
the Brownies, had become very Keen on the nursing profession and with the quick
sightedness of all little girls had noticed on a recent visit to the local hospital
that the nurses wore watches on their clothes and them some of them even wore
a medal on their left tit, or as she put it "On their Jacksies Dad".   To cut
a long story short her next birthday present was a nurses uniform, complete with
carving knife, saw, and entire medical torture set - only one thing was missing,
a medal like the real nurses have, and where better to get one from than the
glass case.   All went well for many weeks of dedicated nursing, carried out on
the patient dolls and on the odd occasion on our long-suffering, much bandaged
an splinted/tied up boxer dog, until at last the sad day came when all nursing
failed and one of the dolls (Walking Talking Chatty Kathy from three Christmas
past), had a full seam and departed this life.   At the time of this unhappy
event I was on patrol in HMS REPULSE, and although I was informed of the medical
failure and subsequent bereavement by family gram I had other things on my mind
and did not mourn too long for Chatty Kathy.   Immediately on my return to harbour
I moved into a house I had purchased in Worcester, my wife having packed, etc,
in my absence, it was not until the second week of my leave that I noticed that
the glass case did not contain my medal.   On asking my wife where the medal was
(Divisions were looming), she said she thought I had taken it to sea with me,
(typical stupid excuse), and began casting "don't say I didn't warn you glances"
at the brat.   After threats, bribery, and a final speech informing them that
should I not be able to find the medal I should be disrated, flogged and court-
martialled prior to being sent back to Borneo to earn another one, and that would
take some time as I would have to wait for another war to start, and I wouldn't get
paid while I was waiting the horrible truth finally emerged.

4.   In the several weeks of agony suffered by poor Kathy prior to her untimely demise, she had not so much as uttered a complaining word, but suffered in silence to the bitter end (not suprising, I had removed the talking bit on Boxing day after the three thousanth "Da Da Sqeak Squeak" etc), she was deemed by the family, the neigbours and no doubt approved by the dog to have been an extremely brave doll, and worthy of recognition.   What better way to recognise the heroism of a dying doll than by lending her Daddies medal that he got from his submarine in Singapore "when the nasty men were going to come and shoot us".   This was all well and good but as things are never done by half in my house, the doll had to be given a good Catholic funeral, and that Sir, is what happened to the medal.   It too was given a good Catholic funeral, and it lies now in a grave, amongst the heather on a quiet hillside in Scotland.   There one day it will be found, perhaps, the circumstances of it's finding will remain for ever a mystery.   But that, Sir, will be the finder's problem, not ours.

    Geographical position of Helensburgh Pier; 56'-05"N 4'-44"W.
    Medal bears 350 degrees - 5000 yards from above.

                    I have the honour to be, Sir,

                        your obedient servant,

                        JP GOODBODY
                        Radio Supervisor

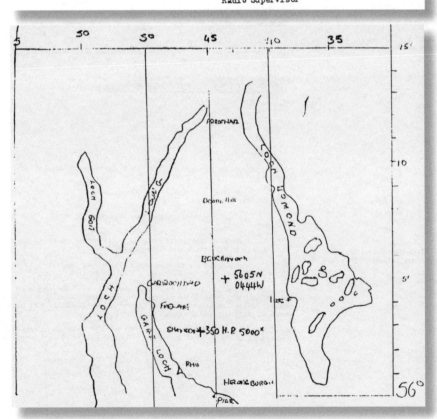

HMS DREADNOUGHT
at Sea

760

The Captain (SM)
Third Submarine Squadron
HMS NEPTUNE

28 October 1973

GOODBODY JP J958924S RADIO SUPERVISOR –
LOSS OF GENERAL SERVICE MEDAL (MALAY PENINSULA)"

1.   The enclosed report is forwarded.

2.   It should be noted that GOODBODY was sufficiently proud of his campaign
service as to want to keep his medal on show.

3.   Although it is realised that the display cabinet should have been kept
locked, it is recommended that sympathetic consideration be given to replacing
the medal from public funds.

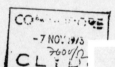

J R B O'RIORDAN
Commander

Enclosure:

1.   Radio Supervisor GOODBODY's

---

5.   FOSNI may, of course, prefer to
medal for outstanding literary merit.

Enclosure:

1.   HMS DREADNOUGHT's letter 760 d
dated 22 October 1973
2.   Chart Tracing

Copy to:

Flag Officer Submarines (for Secretary
The Commanding Officer HMS DREADNOUGH

Office of the Captain SM
Third Submarine Squadron
HMS Neptune
Faslane Helensburgh Dunbartonshire
Telephone Helensburgh 4321 ext

	Your reference
The Flag Officer Scotland and	Our reference 7600/12
Northern Ireland	Date 22 November 1973

GOODBODY J P J958924S RADIO SUPERVISOR –
LOSS OF GENERAL SERVICE MEDAL (MALAY PENINSULA)

Reference:

A. QRRN J 1148

1.   Forwarded.

2.   A replacement from public funds is not considered justified for the following
reasons:

    a.   QRRN were contravened when the shrunken head was initially obtained by the
    swopping of two tots.

    b.   The cupboard containing such an attractive and valuable item should have
    been locked.

    c.   A self-admitted profit was made by the further contraventions of regulations
    when disposing of the head-cigarette box.

    d.   Navigational inaccuracy and geographical ignorance is shown by the
    description of the burial place. (See Enclosure 2)

3.   Had GOODBODY not been of known good character the whole story might well have
been thrown into doubt by the navigational inaccuracy. Granting GOODBODY the
benefit of the doubt, the Commanding Officer HMS DREADNOUGHT will be encouraged to
mount an expedition for the medal's recovery.

4.   In view of the likely condition of the medal if resurrection were achieved,
replacement of the medal is requested; RS GOODBODY to be charged the appropriate
amount.

DESPATCHED

23 NOV 1973

Signature   G.H.

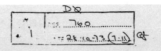

By Sec P

1. This = quite the funniest letter I have read for a long time and I would suggest a copy should be made for the Squadron Line Book.

2. Losses of medals are covered under QRRN J.1148 and replacement from public funds will only be made when the loss of is due to "unavoidable circumstances arising out of the exigencies of the service".

3. DLA.

4. Perhaps NTD can produce a suitable 'replacement'.

—PHONE

DUNFERMLINE 23436] EXT.
INVERKEITHING 2161] 68

TELEX
72322

M.525/2/9

1

Ministry of Defence (NL)

GOODBODY J P J958924S RADIO SUPERVISOR -
LOSS OF GENERAL SERVICE MEDAL (MALAY PENINSULA)

Reference: QRRN J.1148

1.   Forwarded.

2.   The navigational inaccuracy of the burial ground's position has
been noted; the absence of any marker at the graveside makes the
likelihood of successful recovery by an expedition mounted by
HMS DREADNOUGHT unlikely.

3.   Since the loss of medal is clearly covered by the reference as
'an accident of private life' (though Walking Talking Chatty Kathy
might consider the situation somewhat more permanent,) it is
considered that R S GOODBODY must bear the entire cost of replacement
from the profits made from his original disposal of the trophy
cupboard.

4.   Naval Law Division is requested to decide whether replacement may
be made at public expense or not.

5.   HMS DREADNOUGHT is requested to forward the certificate required
by paragraph 1 of the Reference direct to MOD (NL).

COMMUNICATION OFFICE
7600/12
13 DEC 1973
H.M.S. NEPTUNE

R KIRKBY
Commander Royal Navy
for Rear-Admiral

Enclosure: The Captain Third Submar...
dated 22 November 1973 an...

Copy to:

The Flag Officer Submarines (for Secr...
The Captain Third Submarine Squadron
The Commanding Officer HMS DREADNOUGE...

---

(2). Although this is a 3rd Sqd. matter consider the Commodore should not be deprived of the opportunity (in any idle moment which might occur) of reading this.

J 24/1

By 3.
If the Head of NL. had seen this, I suspect a more frivolous reply would have emerged. D/S is not surprised by this solution!

R 25/1.

Have read.

JK.

25 Jan 76.

Chapter Nine

EAT YOUR HEART OUT ARTHUR C...

JUST WHEN YOU THOUGHT THERE WERE NO MORE TIPS:

- Buy a broken exercise bicycle and strap it down to the floor in your kitchen. For added realism, while you are using it get your wife to say, 'Person making strange banging sound in the kitchen, report to Control Room.'

- Have a fluorescent lamp installed on the bottom of your coffee table and lie under it to read books.

- Check your fridge compressor for 'sound shorts'. For added realism, record results in a dog-eared book kept in your front room. For even more realism, get your wife to countersign the book every week.

- Lockwire the wheel nuts on your car.

- When making cakes, prop up one side of the pan while it is baking. Then spread off-white icing really thick on one side to level off the top.

Can you see him?

Occasionally, a submarine magazine would get a scoop. The picture above appeared on the towed array repeat on board HMS *Resolution* on 27 May 1995 at midnight.

The display is normally two bands of random dots, similar to the bottom half of the picture. On the night in question, spookily at midnight, the top channel cleared and the little man appeared. He stayed there for fifteen minutes then the line cleared and resumed its normal appearance. As I said, 'Eat your heart...'

EPILOGUE

While I was compiling this book, I tried to get some recent copies of the boats' magazines, only to be told that they are now banned. It seems the powers that be were worried about 'hurting' people's feelings. How politically correct is that? The boat carries more destructive power than all the bombs dropped in the Second World War, and they're worried about hurting somebody's feelings. Is it just me, or is there something vaguely ironic in that?

I am sure the boats still have magazines, although nowadays they have probably gone underground, or whatever the underwater equivalent is. Hopefully they will re-emerge in the not too distant future, when times are perhaps not so politically correct. Apart from the entertainment value, they had an important social function, a voice for the masses that were often unheard. Quite how the half-truths, downright and blatant lies that made up the ships' magazines levelled the balance I'm not quite sure, but level it they seemed to do.

Countless friendships are formed on board submarines, some that are destined to last a lifetime, some just for the length of a draft, but all of these relationships were formed by the special 'esprit de corps' which is peculiar to the submarine service. They are all professional men who learn to live and work together within the confines of a submarine. They learn to tolerate each other's failings and trust in each other.

The Submariners Association provides a sort of workshop where these very special friendships can be maintained, occasionally repaired and, more importantly, new friendships built. These friendships pay little attention to age, country or even language. Submariners are submariners regardless of age, rank or nationality; a strange category of men, with a somewhat warped outlook on life and a weird sense of humour. The ability for man to live in such close proximity to his fellow man calls for tolerance, open-mindedness, fortitude and a great deal of self-control, and once learnt these lessons last a lifetime.

Whether or not this book helps the reader understand the isolated environment the submariner occupies, or indeed the submariner himself, is open to debate, but I hope at least it provides some insight into his strange and unfamiliar world and, more particularly, how he deals with it.